The Codependency Recovery Plan

THE
CODEPENDENCY
RECOVERY
PLAN

A 5-STEP GUIDE
to Understand, Accept, and Break Free
from the Codependent Cycle

KRYSTAL MAZZOLA, MEd, LMFT

ALTHEA
PRESS

Cover and Interior Designer: Emma Hall
Photo Art Director / Art Manager: Sue Bischofberger
Editor: Nana K. Twumasi
Production Editor: Erum Khan
Author photo courtesy of Orcatek Photography

ISBN: Print 978-1-64152-083-6 | eBook 978-1-64152-084-3

To my mother: There are no words for how blessed I feel
that our relationship is stronger and healthier than I ever
imagined. Thank you so much for focusing on your own
healing—so I could do the same—and thank you for
your unwavering support of me so I could accomplish
my dreams.

Contents

Introduction

Getting to the place in my life where I was ready to write
a book on codependency was a culmination of years spent
learning, helping others recover, and personally becoming
interdependent myself. My family has struggled with codependency multigenerationally (long before we as a society had the
language to describe what was happening). I personally grew
up in an alcoholic and abusive home. Because my mother, who
had me as a teenager, was fixated on pleasing her own emotionally demanding and critical mother—as well as placating
my ex-stepfather, who was the financial provider—there were
no boundaries to protect me from the abuse at home. Both my
mother and my grandmother modeled that cruelty is permissi-
ble so long as the perpetrator meets your basic needs of food,
shelter, and clothing. As a child I would comment at times on
what I saw as inappropriate, confusing, or cruel. I didn't think
telling the truth was brave or foolish; I was just driven to speak
out. However, I was reproached for my desire to "air dirty laun-
dry" within the family. The pain of being treated as a scapegoat
led me to eventually understand that I was expected to stay
silent at any cost to keep others comfortable.

Having my voice seen as burdensome led me to believe that
I was bad, worthless, and unlovable. It took me many years to
reclaim my voice and discover my inherent worth. Prior to my

recovery, the depressing landscape of my codependency led me to contemplate suicide for many years and to attract numerous abusive relationships into my life because I felt I was worth so little. I didn't know exactly how, but there was a driving force inside of me that was committed to healing. I felt it was truly possible to break the patterns of abuse and disempowerment; I just needed to find my way out. My recovery began over 10 years ago, when I began to reconnect with my sense of self through traditional therapy, massage therapy, reiki, and journaling. This process deepened as I developed a meditation practice, began to care for my body through healthy eating and exercise, and prioritized connecting more with others in my life.

Helping myself and others heal became my life's mission. I was compelled to become a couples and family therapist because I knew intimately that our closest relationships greatly impact our sense of self and ability to have a happy life. My personal experience sparked an emerging interest in and understanding of how codependency can fundamentally impact quality of life, self-confidence, and the ability to connect with others, but it was my training and work at The Meadows with Pia Mellody that solidified my choice to focus on this area. During my time guiding people through the Survivors Workshop at The Meadows to address childhood trauma, I realized that the symptoms of codependency—namely, not knowing, liking, or trusting the self—lead to incredible pain and self-destructive tendencies.

Early in my career as a therapist, I believed (inaccurately) that we heal by discussing our problems until something inside us breaks open and, magically, we are whole. However, after working with my first clients, I realized that while naming the problem helps us begin to outline a road map toward healing, it does not do the work of healing for us. Many of us are very good at describing our problems, but often this leads us to feel stuck and powerless. Talking about solutions and positive options is more effective than continually talking about what's wrong. It was with this understanding that I wrote this book. The first two chapters discuss the history of codependency, its symptoms, and the factors that contribute to its development, and the rest of the book details your pathway out.

While you read this book, you may find yourself feeling angry about situations, family dynamics, or cultural narratives in your life that contributed to your belief that you must stay small and quiet, which may have led to the development of your codependency. It is very important to allow yourself to feel this anger but then to remember that you have options now. Entering recovery is about claiming your personal sense of power in this world, as you truly are capable of changing your life, your relationship with yourself, and even many of the relationships with others in your life.

I know taking the first steps can be intimidating, like walking into a dark forest. However, we are walking this path together, and I will hold the flashlight for us. I have learned both personally and with numerous clients that these steps truly lead to interdependency. I'm so grateful you have accepted me as a companion on this part of your healing journey. Thank you. I deeply believe in you.

Part One

CODEPENDENCY: AN EDUCATION

Chapter 1
"I Need You to Need Me"

Rose is a 38-year-old nurse who has been in brief relationships but has never been able to find "the one" with whom she can settle down and finally start the family of her dreams. Whenever she has a boyfriend, she spends her time thinking about all the ways she can make his life easier. For example, even though she often works 12-hour shifts, she spends all her free time cooking extra meals and bringing them over to his house. This meal preparation is time-consuming; she will even go without exercise or seeing friends to keep up. She likes to imagine that her boyfriend will come home after a long day and be nourished by her food, all the while thinking how lucky he is to have found Rose. When her last boyfriend ended things after six months, he told her, "You care too much about others." Rose was dumbfounded. How could her endless supply of nurturance be a negative thing?

What Is Codependency?

"So, is this codependency?" I often hear this question from clients in therapy, and it highlights how difficult codependency is to define. However, there is something about the concept that resonates with people. Adding to the confusion around just what exactly codependency means is the fact that it is not included in the *Diagnostic and Statistical Manual of Mental Disorders*, a tool mental health professionals use to understand the diagnosis of psychiatric disorders and their symptoms. Therefore, there remains no definitive explanation of codependency.

It is important to note that while there is public debate around the value of diagnosis in the first place, I do think it's important to be able to label the distressing symptoms that are part of codependency. In their book *The Whole-Brain Child*, Dan J. Siegel and Tina Payne Bryson discuss the power of retelling events children found distressing to help them integrate the memory so it's less painful, a process they call "name it to tame it." The same strategy is effective for codependency. If we can label a painful process or cycle we feel stuck in, we can see the pathway out of it more clearly.

A BRIEF HISTORY

Initially, the symptoms we now include in codependency were identified within the 12-step community circa 1939, about four years after Alcoholics Anonymous was founded, when people began meeting to find ways to improve their relationship with the recovering alcoholic in their life. In 1951, Al-Anon was officially founded as a support community for those who are friends, family members, or partners of someone struggling with alcoholism.

The term *codependent* first emerged in 1979 to describe how life becomes unmanageable for someone in a relationship with an alcoholic. When I first learned of codependency, it was from this original framework. At the time, I was deeply entrenched in my own codependent relationship with an addict. When I read about codependency from this perspective, I immediately thought, "So, it's true—he's the problem!" I did not realize that this was my desperate attempt to deflect and minimize my role in the painful relationship.

In 1986, Melody Beattie introduced the public—those outside of treatment settings—to codependency with her book *Codependent No More*. In that book, Beattie defines the codependent as someone "who has let another person's behavior affect him or her, and who is obsessed with controlling that person's behavior." Over time, she updated this definition. In *The New Codependency*, she states that a codependent overly engages in normal behaviors in relationships, such as caring or doing too much for another person. Of course, it is normal to care about our loved ones. The problem is when the relationship becomes obsessive and controlling. Pia Mellody defines codependency as a disease of immaturity caused by childhood trauma. In this view, the symptoms of codependency prevent people from living functionally in adulthood because they become stuck in less-developed ways of relating to others, such as having no boundaries or struggling to accept imperfection.

Throughout the years, the definition of codependency has expanded significantly, and now we understand that it is a cluster of symptoms that exist whether a codependent person is in a romantic partnership or not. However, until we heal our own codependent symptoms, we will often find ourselves in relationships that are toxic. Many people in codependency often believe that the reason they are caught in these painful relationship cycles is because they just haven't found "the one," rather than realizing they have their own reasons for attracting such relationships in the first place.

Familiar Signs and Symptoms

When we talk about the symptoms of codependency, we are actually referring to a series of behaviors that are meant to help the codependent make sense of feeling powerless and unworthy. It should be restated that we now know codependency does not require addiction. Of course, people in their codependency are often in a lot of pain, and some choose to numb this pain with drugs, alcohol, or food. However, if this numbing behavior subsides rather readily once the codependency is addressed, then this is separate from true addiction, which is seen as a disease.

Below, I have outlined the five core domains of codependency from my clinical perspective, along with the various symptoms within these domains. All might not relate to your life. Regardless, I invite you to go through this list and identify the ways you can relate.

THE NEED TO PLEASE PEOPLE

You prioritize others' approval and desire over what you want or need, and you may not even know what you want or need. You may:

- Believe you are selfish if you focus on yourself at all

- Feel guilt when you say no

- Experience resentment when people don't appreciate all that you do for them (even when they didn't ask for your support)

The Definition of Codependency

I define codependency as prioritizing others' needs, expectations, or problems over one's own mental and physical health. In codependency, a person's sense of worth comes from others rather than internally. Codependent individuals do not believe in their inherent value, so they need external measures to prove their worth. With this definition, we can see that Rose is codependent, as her desire to keep a partner is more important to her than anything else. The goal of recovery is interdependency, where a person can care and nurture others but never to one's own personal detriment. We can see that Rose neglects herself, by not seeing friends or exercising, to take care of her boyfriend in the hope that he will choose to settle down with her, a key symptom of her codependency.

This external focus leads a codependent person to want to control the other person in the relationship. This highlights the fundamental paradox of codependency: The more someone focuses on controlling another, the more out of control they feel, since no person can change another. This paradox leads them to feel powerless and victimized.

Codependency is a pervasive experience; it is a lens through which one sees the people in one's life. In codependency, emotional experience is often reduced to feelings of fear or anxiety ("I'm not safe"), resentment ("You should be the way I want you to be"), guilt

("I can't say no or I'm bad"), and shame ("I'm not worthwhile or lovable"). Furthermore, people with codependency have this disorder whether they are in a relationship or not. It exists within them.

Codependent relationships are inherently imbalanced. Usually there is someone who gives beyond what is appropriate, reasonable, or honest, and there is someone who takes inappropriately. In this book, I will focus on the traits and needs for recovery of those who overly give to prove their worth. The more demanding and selfish (more narcissistic) presentation of codependency is complex and deserves special and separate discussion. To avoid complication, I will focus on the recovery path of those who are more passive and giving.

- Want to avoid all conflict even if it means giving up what's important to you

- Give power away, believe someone else has a better idea of how to live your life, or feel hostage to others' expectations

- Believe your emotions or needs are a burden to others

- Struggle to focus on your own issues

- Believe that you must live up to someone else's standards rather than your own

LACK OF SELF-AWARENESS AND SENSE OF SELF-WORTH

You have a sense that you do not know who you really are or that you have lost yourself. You regard yourself in terms of the roles you serve for others. You may:

- Pin your worth on the judgment of others

- Strive to perform to prove your worth

- Discredit personal accomplishments

- Complete goals but move on to setting a new goal rather than enjoying your achievement

- Be willing to change your interests depending on whom you spend time with

- Sense that you have lost yourself or never knew who you really were in the first place

- Have the desire to die, disappear, or not exist—maybe due to the pain of codependency—to get others to finally appreciate you

REALITY ISSUES

You struggle with your individual perspective on the world and have trouble clarifying your thoughts, feelings, needs, and sense of self. You may:

- Accept others' version of reality over your own

- Feel bad, sick, or wrong when second-guessing others

- Dissociate from reality, sometimes by numbing the self with alcohol, drugs, pornography, food, excessive shopping, or work

- Minimize how things are impacting you

- Have trouble understanding how you feel about events in your life

DISTORTED THINKING

You have a tendency to experience generalized and negative thoughts about yourself, others, and the world. You may:

- Believe that it's not okay or safe to share what you truly think or feel

- Take others' behavior personally

- Struggle with perfectionism

- Experience "all-or-nothing" thinking

- Struggle with obsessive worry and can't let go of thoughts

- Be convinced you know how other people should truly be

- Not accept others for who they actually are

- Engage in magical thinking, like if only the other person would change, then everything in your life would be perfect

INTIMACY ISSUES

You may struggle to maintain relationships, feel overwhelmed when others want to get to know you, or often feel invisible to others. You may:

- Have the sense of desperately wanting to be one with someone

- Turn someone else into your God or oxygen

- Bottle up feelings until you explode and feel justified because you have stayed quiet for so long

- Feel abandoned when others set limits with you, such as needing a break from a conversation

- Allow others to dominate conversations and plans so that you can hide behind them

EXERCISE: Codependency Questionnaire

At this point, you have gained an understanding of the symptoms of codependency but may still be confused as to how these symptoms apply to you. This questionnaire was designed with common experiences in codependency in mind to help clarify how you may personally experience codependency.

Check any statements you agree with.

☐ I have been told that I'm controlling.

☐ When I think about my problems, I feel guilty. After all, there are so many other people struggling with much more serious problems than mine—who am I to complain?

☐ Sometimes it feels like I don't know what to talk about if I'm not talking about the person whom I feel dependent on.

- ☐ I can give someone many chances to finally meet my needs and will still acquiesce when they yet again violate me.

- ☐ I don't know who I truly am outside of my roles in my life (e.g., daughter, wife, employee).

- ☐ I'm desperately afraid of ending up alone.

- ☐ Sometimes it feels like my life is on hold and I'm waiting for my "real life" to begin.

- ☐ It is common for me to say yes when I want to say no.

- ☐ I spend time with people I dislike just so I have company.

- ☐ I resent when I give others advice and they don't take it.

- ☐ If I sense a problem in my relationship, I am quick to believe that I am the problem, or the way I perceive things is the problem, rather than explore other reasons for the issues between me and the other person.

- ☐ I avoid asking others for help because I cannot risk their saying no.

- ☐ Growing up, I focused on earning praise for my grades and/ or athletic abilities.

- ☐ I never heard "I love you" by one of my parents when I was growing up.

- ☐ I cannot tolerate when someone is mad at me and obsess about how to make them happy again, even if it means I go back on what's important to me.

- ☐ If someone I care about feels something, I often feel the same thing. I cannot rest until they feel okay again.

- ☐ When someone I love makes a mistake, I feel personally responsible for their actions.

☐ I hold back on telling someone what I feel or need because I don't want to be a burden.

☐ My mind often goes blank when people ask me what I like or want.

☐ I often find myself defending my loved one's behavior as "not that bad" to my friends and family.

☐ I have felt grateful when someone chooses to spend time with me.

☐ I feel like things are boring if there's not chaos, drama, or a crisis.

☐ I have gone along with a loved one's story of an event and told myself repeatedly how wrong I am when my gut nagged at me that it wasn't true.

☐ I have fantasized about something bad happening to me, like a serious car accident, so the people in my life will finally appreciate me and all that I do for them.

☐ If someone I'm in a relationship with tells me something about who they are or what they value that seriously concerns me, I actively try to forget it or believe they will change.

☐ Although I have no medical reason for it, I am frequently sick.

☐ I give "subtle" hints on how someone could change to better fit what makes me comfortable, such as leaving brochures on recovery or weight loss around the house.

☐ Throughout my childhood, there were emotions or behaviors that were unacceptable or mocked, such as crying or being angry.

☐ Growing up, I was often told by the adults in my life comments like "No, you don't really think that" or "No, that's not how you feel" when I would share my thoughts or feelings.

□ I have been told "I never asked you to do that" when I shared my upset that someone wasn't grateful for something I did for them.

□ Growing up, I was blamed for things I didn't do or had no control over, such as my parents fighting.

□ I feel overwhelmed and anxious if the person I'm dating takes a while to respond to a message, to the point that it's very difficult for me to focus on my own life.

□ Growing up, there were some topics that were "off-limits."

□ I avoid buying myself items even when necessary, like cold-weather clothing, because caring for myself feels frivolous, unimportant, or tedious.

□ I anticipate what I think others want from me and interact with them based on this calculation rather than what is true for me.

Please count all your check marks to find your score:

0–8: You do not often question your worth and, overall, have healthy and authentic relationships.

9–18: You likely had at least a few shaming experiences growing up that make you second-guess your worth and the validity of your needs and feelings now. You may not be struggling fully in codependency, but you will likely still benefit from following the guidelines of recovery in this book, such as setting boundaries.

19 OR MORE: You are likely struggling with codependency, so congratulations on picking up this book! This is a step toward self-care, which should be celebrated. Please follow along with this book and complete the exercises to begin your recovery work. Healing truly is possible!

A Troubled Childhood

Initially, the development of codependency was thought to occur when someone was raised in an alcoholic or addicted household. However, a study by Julie Fuller and Rebecca Warner, researchers at the University of New Hampshire, revealed that codependency can develop in any family with high levels of stress, which can involve alcoholism but may include other stressors, as well, such as having a family member with a chronic illness or serious mental health issues. Abuse may or may not be present. It appears that growing up in a troubled family is a major contributor to feeling devalued and disempowered, which sets a person up for codependency.

Pioneering family therapist Virginia Satir noticed there are just a few main differences between healthy and troubled families. These differences center on self-worth, family rules, and communication. In a healthy family, there are realistic and flexible expectations. According to Satir, in troubled families, the self-worth of the members is low and communication is unclear and dishonest. Satir's definition of a troubled family aligns with the theory that codependency originates from trauma. It's worthwhile to note that the word *trauma* comes from a Greek word meaning "wound." Many of us can identify some wounds from our childhood, even if they were completely inadvertent on the part of our families.

INVALIDATION

Many codependents grew up in an environment where their truth was not supported. This may happen in a family in which children are not expected to be heard or are expected to stifle their emotions or perspectives to keep their parents comfortable. For example, a child may be hurt by a parent's criticism, and the

other parent may say that's just how the parent expresses love—
that the child's way of interpreting the situation is wrong.

SWALLOWING EMOTIONS

In some families, children are taught to hide their emotions.
For example, many of my clients, when they were children,
internalized the message that crying is weak. This message can
be indirect, such as a scornful look, or it may be more obvious,
such as being told crying is for wimps or being threatened, "If
you don't stop crying, I'll give you something to cry about."
These experiences can rob children of feeling connected to
their voice as they grow up. Furthermore, swallowing emotions
also creates issues with knowing and asserting one's reality.

DENYING THE SENSE OF SELF

Children in troubled families can experience not only the min-
imization of their views and emotions but also the invalidation
of their core sense of self. This happens when children are not
only sent the message that their thoughts or feelings wrong, but
also that who they are fundamentally is a problem. Growing
up, it was common for my mother to tell me, "Krystal, I love
you but I don't like you." This communicated to me that I'm
inherently broken and unlikable. If my own mother didn't like
me, I must be unlovable. Similar messages may have been sent
through statements like "What's wrong with you?" whenever
you made a mistake.

UNREALISTIC EXPECTATIONS

Troubled families also tend to have unrealistic and rigid expectations. We'll take a closer look at this in the next chapter, but
in these situations, the family expects the child to behave like
a little adult in all situations. An example is taking a toddler to

a fancy restaurant and getting angry with the child for crying or being troublesome in public. Perhaps your family expected straight As, no matter what. Put simply, this involves any expectation of perfection. As we know, no human being is perfect.

NEGLECT OR ABANDONMENT

The experience of neglect or abandonment can set us up for codependency. Children have a limited understanding of the world that leads them to believe that if awful things happen, it's because of who they are. When we mature, we learn that others' actions represent their character rather than our personal character, but children are unable to understand this. Therefore, when a caregiver abandons or neglects a child, the child believes that being bad, or not good enough, caused the caregiver's abandonment. If only they had been better, their caregiver would have stayed, is the false belief that arises from this experience.

It is important to note that a parent can be physically present but still emotionally neglectful. Consider a child who discloses sexual abuse, but the family denies it could have happened.

Not every person experiencing codependency had a troubled childhood. Sometimes the development of codependency occurs in adulthood. In these cases, it appears to be caused by an attachment injury, like being abandoned or betrayed by a loved one in a time of serious need, such as when an affair occurs while one partner is grievously ill, or domestic abuse. Regardless of when you developed your codependency, your feelings are valid.

The act of journaling puts us in touch with our true views, emotions, and needs. It is a fundamental component of healing from codependency, which is why I encourage you to keep a journal. Keep it on hand as you work through this book.

For your first journal entry, write about any of the feelings that are coming up for you as you learn more about codependency and your personal symptoms. It is common to feel sadness, resentment, and embarrassment. Write about any new insights you may be having at this time about yourself, your family, or your other relationships. Finally, please write what you think about changing these patterns in your life.

Coexisting Conditions

Codependency is not itself a mental illness, but it can and often does coexist with mental health issues. Psychiatric disorders—unlike codependency—have a physiological and genetic component. Studies using MRI brain scans show that the brains of those without psychiatric disorders appear different than those with issues such as depression or bipolar disorder. A study by Drs. Youjin Zhao and Su Lui showed that in regard to both major depressive disorder (MDD) and social anxiety disorder (SAD), those affected have a thicker insular cortex, which impacts self-awareness and perception, as well as a thicker anterior cingulate cortex, which is linked to emotion. The study showed that people with SAD have brains that were structurally different in the areas that process fear. People with MDD had structural differences in their visual recognition network.

Impairments in this area may explain issues with focus, memory, and recognizing others' emotions by their facial expressions.

Codependency can also exist alongside concerns such as eating disorders, including anorexia, bulimia, and binge-eating disorder. Furthermore, while codependency can develop without the presence of addiction, some people struggle with a substance-abuse problem or addiction as well as codependency. Addiction is diagnosed when the behavior or substance is increasingly important despite actual or potential consequences—such as the inability to go to work, loss of money, or legal issues—and when you have problems staying abstinent from the behavior or substance for long periods of time even when there are compelling reasons to abstain, such as an ultimatum by a partner you love.

If you believe, after reviewing the symptoms and questionnaires in this book, that you have numerous symptoms or concerns that were not addressed, it could be useful to meet with a psychiatrist. The first appointment with a psychiatrist is an interview to gather more information about your symptoms to clarify whether you have a mental health issue. This can be an intimidating process, but remember, you have to name it to tame it. If you know more about what you are experiencing outside of codependency, you can work with others, such as a mental health professional, or gather other resources, such as workbooks, to guide your concurrent recovery process. Furthermore, there are specialized resources for these concerns, such as 12-step programs for substance abuse and eating disorders. It is highly recommended to seek medical care as well if you are experiencing an eating disorder, as there are many associated health risks, including higher mortality rates.

Finally, if you have a coexisting condition, it is still valuable to recover from codependency. After all, living with codependency is very stressful, and stress often exacerbates

On the 12 Steps

While many people have found healing from codependency with the 12 steps, this book does not follow those steps. However, attendance at meetings such as Al-Anon (for those close to someone with a dependence on any kind of substance, not just alcohol), Sex and Love Addicts Anonymous (SLAA), or Co-dependents Anonymous (CODA) can be a good supplement to this book. If you are interested in learning more, many communities have their own meetings. The best way to find local meetings is through the organization's website, such as Al-Anon.org. Books may also guide you through the 12 steps, such as *A Gentle Path through the Twelve Steps*, by Patrick Carnes, and *Codependents' Guide to the Twelve Steps*, by Melody Beattie.

mental health disorders. While I cannot speak to the brain changes in my clients, I've observed that their mental health symptoms, such as those caused by depression, addiction, or post-traumatic stress disorder, become a lot more manageable when they become interdependent. In interdependency, they value their care more, so they are more likely to practice important coping skills to stay more stable and seek support as needed if their symptoms are intense at times.

Your Path Forward

The goal of this book is to help you in your journey to recover from codependency. As someone who has a personal and professional stake in the issue, I fully believe recovery is a lifestyle you can learn to live. As you read through this book, you will learn ways to discover or reconnect with who you authentically are and care for yourself. You will learn how to protect yourself with healthy boundaries. Finally, you will learn how to have healthy relationships with clear and honest communication, which will pave the way for a deeper sense of intimacy in your life than you have known before.

EXERCISE: A Simple Meditation

Mindfulness is about giving full attention to the present moment without judgment. It is noticing and accepting the present for what it is at any given moment. Learning how to quiet our mind through mindfulness has incredible benefits: It helps us reduce anxiety and let go of obsessive thinking, increases our awareness of who we are, and reduces our impulse to react to things out of intense emotion, among other benefits.

The simplest way to begin a mindfulness practice is to learn how to connect with the breath. Eckhart Tolle, spiritual teacher and author, says, "Whenever you are conscious of the breath, you are absolutely present." Many of us in our codependency experience an onslaught of thoughts, both obsessive and self-critical. Mindfulness slows this process down.

To begin, find a quiet place where you will not be bothered for at least a few minutes, and sit comfortably with your back upright. Take a few normal breaths to center yourself. Take a deep breath through your nose, hold it, and then slowly relax your jaw and release the breath through your mouth. Begin to breathe in deeply through the nose and, with this inhalation, imagine you can pull in a sense of peace or relaxation. Hold the breath for a moment. When you breathe out, imagine all tension in your body and mind can be pushed out of you with your exhalation. If your mind wanders, just come back to your breath—this is the practice of mindfulness, returning to the present. Continue to breathe in this manner for four cycles and then pause. You have done great work today. Notice how your mind and body feel after this exercise.

Continue this practice whenever you can throughout your day to center and calm yourself.

It's Okay to Care

As humans, we seek connection. Research shows that loneliness and social isolation can increase the risk for premature death. The healthy alternative to codependency is not total independence and isolation; rather, it is interdependence. When interdependent, we are responsible to care for our own emotional, physical, and financial health while simultaneously accepting support from others as needed.

Consider this simple example of interdependency at play: If you are moving, you are responsible to find your next residence, pack up your items, and move into your new place, but you will also need support, maybe by working with a real estate agent or asking friends to help you move. It is not wise to attempt a move completely alone. Put simply, when we are interdependent, we give from an authentic, generous space rather than one of obligation, and we accept support from others for the things we cannot do for ourselves.

TAKE IT FURTHER

Codependency can have a range of definitions, but this book will apply the definition that codependency is characterized by an external focus rather than an internal focus to measure self-worth. In this chapter, you have been invited to notice your own symptoms.

Prior to moving on to the next chapter, please consider the following:

1. Compliment yourself for picking up this book—this was a courageous act of self-care.

2. Practice self-compassion. It is common to have some feelings of shame come up as you inspect your behaviors, but they have come from an honest place of pain in your past. Oprah Winfrey has said that Maya Angelou told her, "When you know better, you do better."

3. Consider your reactions to the encouragement to begin a mindfulness practice. It is common to feel resistance—you may feel you don't have time for it or don't know how to do it. Notice your resistance if it's there, honor it, but continue with learning how to connect with your breath. What do you have to lose?

Chapter 2
Family Matters

Carrie, 46, and her mother, 73, have always been very close. When Carrie was growing up, they took great pride in telling others that they were best friends. Her mother would always brag that no one was a better daughter than Carrie. However, in her relationships with others, Carrie struggles with feeling comfortable if people do not compliment her or remind her that she's important to them, because she grew up associating her worth with the frequent compliments given by her mother. These days, her mother's health is beginning to decline, and Carrie feels a lot of pressure to be the perfect caregiver for her. This is complicated by the fact that when Carrie has other obligations, her mother guilt-trips her by suggesting that they don't know how much time they have together and that Carrie must have other priorities. Carrie once suggested they hire a part-time caregiver to help when Carrie is at work, but her mother became offended that Carrie wanted to pass her off to a stranger. Her mother has become increasingly critical and withholding of compliments, so Carrie is uncertain if she is doing a good job as a caregiver, which is impacting her self-esteem. Carrie is motivated to do better, so after working a long day, she goes to her mother's house and prepares meals, helps bathe her, and administers her medications. She also prepares everything her mother will need for the next day when she's at work. It is common now for Carrie to sleep only five hours a night, which is impacting her mood and energy. She's also noticed a cough that won't go away, but she doesn't have time right now to go to the doctor for herself.

Dysfunctional Family Archetypes

As mentioned in chapter 1, our early experiences can greatly contribute to the development of codependency. Some troubled families set rigid, yet unspoken, rules related to the concept of family roles. Virginia Satir, whom I introduced previously, first identified these roles, which are expected ways of being for each family member. Addiction specialist Claudia Black and Sharon Wegsheider-Cruse, founder of the National Association for Children of Alcoholics, both expanded on these roles to fit alcoholic families. Their work significantly contributed to the initial understanding of codependency. To better understand the impact of roles on family functioning, it is important to look at family systems theory. Most family therapists view families as a system in which the whole is greater than the sum of its parts. In troubled families, there is often some rigidity in the ways the parts perform, and as such, we can see that roles serve a purpose in maintaining the dysfunctional family system. It is important to note that while the term *dysfunctional* may feel stigmatizing, from a family systems perspective, it simply refers to a family that is not functioning well. In a functional family, adults and children are allowed their own viewpoints, emotions, and sense of self, and there are clear expectations for and consequences of behaviors.

In a family system, homeostasis is whatever a given family views as the status quo, which can then be interpreted as stability—even if it is chaotic. It is not uncommon for other family members to exhibit behaviors that sabotage mental health or addiction recovery because of this homeostasis. This is what first alerted mental health professionals that there was another dysfunctional process at play in an addicted family, not just the addiction itself. Finally, roles become complementary. We need one another to stick to the script so that the family can maintain its balance. It should be noted that the healthier a family is, the less rigid these roles are, whereas the more stressed a family, the more fixed the roles. For example, Carrie has always been expected to be the "perfect daughter," which is a rigid role. Carrie may truly value caring for others, including her mother, but her mother's approval is dependent on Carrie performing perfectly in caring for her mother, even as Carrie's life circumstances change.

It is important to note that you may have been placed into different roles by different sets of circumstances. Maybe you were the "Hero" until your mother died, but when your father remarried, you became the "Scapegoat." These changes can further complicate our sense of self and self-worth. Let's discuss the common codependent family roles.

THE ENABLER

As a child, the Enabler may have learned to stifle their own concerns and feelings in order to support other family members. They deny, avoid, and dissociate from their own anger. In families or couples struggling with addiction or serious untreated mental illness, the Enabler is the person who protects loved ones from the natural consequences of their behaviors. Therefore, growing up, the Enabler often struggles with knowing how to be assertive. In a family, this child is expected sometimes to be a surrogate parent for the parent. But, as we know, it's unrealistic to think a child is equipped to function as an adult. No child can be all-supportive and totally present. Frankly, no adult can meet this task, either. Therefore, the Enabler will internalize shame for not being perfect in their ability to care for others.

THE HERO

The Hero is often seen as the child incapable of doing any wrong. But when the Hero makes a mistake, the family either has an unconscious agreement to not acknowledge it or places the blame on the Scapegoat (page 28). For example, the Hero would never abuse drugs if it hadn't been for the Scapegoat forcing them to do so. It is common for the other children to feel jealous and resentful of the Hero.

The Hero grows up receiving praise for their accomplishments and abilities or even their physical attributes. This is in place of praise for their true character. The Hero learns that they must always be charming and pleasing because it's their responsibility to keep the family happy through a sense of pride. It is important to note that the Hero also learns that the rules in the family do not apply to them in the same way as others. They learn they are capable of undermining structure to meet their own needs. For example, this may happen when they go to one parent with a request and are told no, but the other parent chooses to tell them yes, even when this never happens for their siblings. This reinforces the idea to the Hero that they are special and the rules are different for them.

THE SCAPEGOAT

The Scapegoat is often used to center the family's anger and hostility as a way of reducing conflict among other family members. After all, with the Scapegoat, everyone has one person to target as the source for all that ails the family. The Scapegoat is often the truth teller in the family. They may be the child who tells a teacher that there is abuse or addiction in the home.

The Scapegoat learns they are bad and that they can earn attention for negative behavior. Often, the Scapegoat is rebellious. Perhaps they don't do well in school or they act out in other ways, such as early sexual activity and drug use. It should be noted that the Scapegoat can do well in school or other activities, but their accomplishments are not celebrated in the way that the Hero's would be. Furthermore, they can struggle to express anger in moderate ways and may even have tantrums through adolescence and in their adulthood.

This role is often fulfilled by an addict. The addict may be an adult in the family, and the general belief among other family members is that if the addict would just recover, then all the family problems would be healed. Of course, the difficulty of this role is that other family members tend to be incredibly defensive against the idea of working to change their own behaviors, too, which continues to contribute to the addiction cycle within the family.

THE LOST CHILD

We can understand the Lost Child as an emotional orphan. They may be largely invisible and neglected by the other family members. The Lost Child's purpose in the family is to be a source of relief, as the general belief is that no one needs to worry about them. This is a very lonely role and often contributes to the Lost Child's thinking that they must deny their own feelings so that they aren't a burden. This role contributes to the development of codependency, as the Lost Child may grow up struggling to know what they need or feel due to this pattern of denial. We learn who we are, in part, from the intimate feedback of our parents or caregivers, and without it, we may feel totally disconnected with our sense of self.

THE MASCOT

Every family needs comic relief, and the Mascot serves this purpose. This person is often seen as weak, dependent, and immature. When a caregiver is anxious, they may look for someone like the Mascot to funnel their anxiety toward; therefore, this person may grow up feeling smothered by intimacy. Growing up with family members or a parent who looks to others to meet all their needs, the Mascot may learn they are not capable on their own. They may feel helpless or incompetent. The Mascot may grow up feeling they cannot rely on themselves even to accomplish basic tasks. The Mascot also learns how to mask their own feelings as a joke, and as a consequence, often others don't take them seriously. This leads to difficulty asserting themselves.

EXERCISE: Identifying Codependent Family Roles

While reading the family roles, you may have noticed strong feelings about or an affinity for different roles for yourself and your family members. In this exercise, you will increase your understanding of how your family has contributed to some of your codependent symptoms.

First, create a timeline from birth to when you left your childhood home. Next, make a list of all your family members or people you lived with growing up. This may include extended family, such as an aunt or a grandparent. On your timeline, note births, deaths, major moves, and separations or divorces to the best of your knowledge. Review the Dysfunctional Family Archetypes (page 25) and then begin to identify the roles you resonate with from your childhood. You may have had one fixed role, or it may have changed over time. Next, do the same for your family members, including any siblings.

Afterward, journal about any thoughts or insights you have. As you notice the roles you have played growing up in your family, practice self-compassion regarding your codependency. You were taught that you could receive love, attention, or acceptance by performing a part for your family rather than being allowed to explore your authentic self. Imagine yourself as a child, and feel compassion for this child and how they were not taught they were worthwhile just as they were.

Codependent Family Relationships

From a family systems perspective, the whole family behaves in either a functional or a dysfunctional manner, but in regard to troubled family relationships, some can be more overtly codependent than others. Here are some ways these relationships manifest.

PARENT–PARENT OR PARENT–PARTNER

You may have a parent who is codependent on their partner. This situation can occur when there is an addict parent and an Enabler (page 26), or it may exist without addiction if one parent is fixated on keeping their partner happy at all costs. In a healthy family, the focus is on the children, as they are not yet capable of fully meeting their own needs. However, in this scenario, the adults are more focused on themselves and one another instead of the children.

PARENT–CHILD

In this relationship, a parent subconsciously uses their child to meet their own needs—when, of course, the opposite should be true. An example is a woman who is driven to have a child so she can finally have someone who loves her and will not "abandon" her (*abandon* is in quotes here because as an adult, she can meet her own needs, and it is the task of the child to eventually mature to find their own path in life). This scenario may also exist in an adult child–parent relationship. For example, Carrie's mother expects Carrie to be her sole caregiver. In an interdependent relationship, although Carrie's mother may want more time with her daughter, she would be able to recognize that Carrie must work to support herself and cannot be available to her constantly, and they could discuss hiring a part-time caregiver.

This situation can also manifest in a family where a parent is struggling with addiction or mental illness, and a child may need to take over household responsibilities. Perhaps they are the oldest child who helps all the other children with their homework and gets them fed because their parent is literally, or emotionally, absent.

SIBLING–SIBLING

In my experience, this is a more rare presentation of codependency, as it is parents who typically reinforce codependent roles among children. In a codependent sibling relationship, there is a sense of deep responsibility to the sibling. Sometimes this happens in the case of twins or multiple births. Another example may be when one of two siblings is healthy and the other is chronically ill—the healthy child may be raised to feel guilty and responsible for the ill sibling. Finally, it's also common for siblings who are much older to have more of a surrogate-parent type of relationship with their younger siblings.

Address Your Fears

When we begin to contemplate setting boundaries around our family roles so that we may live more authentically, we may discover that we feel incapable or overwhelmed by the idea of changing. As we begin to break away from our codependency, we may feel attached to it because it offers a sense of predictability. Many of us have created numerous ways of behaving that reinforce our role. In letting go of our role, we need to change deeply ingrained behaviors, set boundaries around our family, and begin to discover who we authentically are. While the benefits of this change will eventually reduce our pain, stress, and sense of exhaustion, it is very normal to feel nervous when beginning to contemplate stepping outside our role.

INFERIORITY

In the process of discovering who we truly are outside of our family role, we may notice feelings of shame—the emotion that tells us we're not enough to be loved or appreciated in our authentic self. Performing a role for our family can be incredibly draining, but at least in our role, we know we are depended on for something. Carrie's mother instilled in her from a young age that she is worthwhile for being kind and well-behaved. Because of this, Carrie may be afraid to break out of her role as the perfect daughter because she is unsure she has worth if she can't always meet her mother's needs or wants.

When we feel that our worth is dependent on being needed by others, the thought of becoming authentic is terrifying because we don't know yet if we will be loved or valued just for being. When we are afraid we are worth less than other people, we may feel we have to prove our value to stay in a relationship with others.

ABANDONMENT

Fear of abandonment is connected to the feeling of not being good enough, especially if we feel somehow unfit to be our authentic self. We may believe those in our lives want us around only if we are doing things for them or taking care of them because we don't trust we have inherent value. While roles may confuse us, there are certainly people who will be happy to become closer to you. There are people who want to know the real you—not the mask you hide behind out of fear of being worthless. That may be scary to consider, but take a moment to think about the people you love, and contemplate: Do you want them to pretend to be someone they are not for your comfort, or do you, in your heart of hearts, want to know them honestly? I imagine your answer, deep down, is the latter, and the same is true for those who love you.

GUILT

Guilt is a driving motivator for many to stay in their codependency. Guilt is the feeling that we must do things for others out of duty or obligation and to prove love or worth, even to our own personal detriment. From this viewpoint, it is common to think it is unloving or unkind to set boundaries in our relationships based on our authentic needs. Carrie is overwhelmed by the demands of work and caregiving for her mother, but when her mother objects to the prospect of hiring a part-time caregiver, guilt motivates Carrie to not change. She tells herself that her mother has done so much for her and she should be less selfish, which propels her to stay stuck in the cycle of working, caregiving, and not sleeping enough, even as it is starting to impact her health.

EXERCISE: Breaking Unhelpful Thought Patterns

Through the lens of codependency, it is common to have numerous unhelpful thoughts that contribute to our codependent behaviors and relationships. In cognitive behavioral therapy, these unhelpful thoughts, often labeled "cognitive distortions" or "thinking errors," are replaced by a more balanced assertion. Some examples of unhelpful thoughts appear below; as you read them, please note the ones that resonate with you. Each example includes a more helpful, affirming statement to replace this thought.

UNHELPFUL THOUGHT: I cannot ask others for support; I must do it on my own.

MORE HELPFUL THOUGHT: Learning how to ask others for help puts me in a position of vulnerability. I can learn to tolerate the discomfort of my vulnerability. As I heal from codependency, it is important for me to become interdependent so my needs can be met and I can engage in healthy and connected relationships.

UNHELPFUL THOUGHT: I must repress my feelings and needs to keep others comfortable.

MORE HELPFUL THOUGHT: I have the right to my feelings and needs. I am responsible to share who I am with others in a kind way to prevent resentment that is unfair to the relationship.

UNHELPFUL THOUGHT: It is mean or wrong to set boundaries with others.

MORE HELPFUL THOUGHT: It is unkind to allow myself to feel victimized by someone as it hurts my sense of self-respect and hurts our relationship. Without boundaries, I will ultimately resent the person.

UNHELPFUL THOUGHT: If only I were better, people would change/heal/recover.

MORE HELPFUL THOUGHT: Other people's actions are a reflection of themselves and their values, not a reflection of my personal worth in the world. I am worthwhile even if the people I love are struggling.

UNHELPFUL THOUGHT: I will know I finally matter when a positive event happens.

MORE HELPFUL THOUGHT: Some things may add joy or a sense of purpose to my life, but my life matters and so do I, even without these things.

UNHELPFUL THOUGHT: Everyone must like me.

MORE HELPFUL THOUGHT: It is uncomfortable for other people to not like me and painful to lose important relationships, but I have already survived many painful feelings and I can survive these. While not everyone will accept, like, and love me, there are people in this world who can and will.

UNHELPFUL THOUGHT: I am broken.

MORE HELPFUL THOUGHT: There are reasons I have learned to act the way I have in my relationships with others, and I struggle with caring for myself. But I can have compassion for myself, and I am worthy of love and respect.

UNHELPFUL THOUGHT: If I am not perfect, I am worthless.

MORE HELPFUL THOUGHT: I have strengths and I have flaws just like all other people. We all have things that are worth celebrating and areas of growth. I am capable of embracing my imperfections.

UNHELPFUL THOUGHT: Changing is not worth the work because it is tiring and may impact those I love.

MORE HELPFUL THOUGHT: Living in my codependency has been a lot of work, which I have survived, so I'm capable of doing the work of changing. The comfort of being connected to myself will allow me more joy in my life and will lead to deeper relationships with others.

UNHELPFUL THOUGHT: It is cruel for me to not take care of my loved ones when they are suffering.

MORE HELPFUL THOUGHT: When others I care about are in pain, it is appropriate to feel concern for them, but I must allow them the dignity of feeling their own feelings as well as the potential growth of experiencing their natural consequences.

We will continue this work in a later chapter, so it is valuable to note your thoughts in your journal for later reference. If any of these examples deeply resonate with you, please write out the more helpful statement. You may want to hang it up somewhere you will see the affirmation frequently (such as your bathroom mirror) to begin to challenge that original, unhelpful thought.

Learning to Detach

In Buddhist teachings, the root of all suffering is attachment, or clinging to our desires. In codependency, attachment usually manifests as obsessive worry or a deep belief that we can be happy only if certain things in our life are achieved, like getting a loved one to stay sober or receiving a promotion. This attachment in our codependency is often a compulsive process rather than one we actively choose to engage in. In my codependency, I often felt like a dog with a bone; I just couldn't quit thinking about the object of my obsession. Of course, nothing productive ever came of this fixation.

It can be deeply scary to even contemplate detaching or letting go. After all, if we had a sense of trust that things would be okay, we wouldn't hold on so tightly. In most cases, it does us a disservice to believe that if we hold on to something, we can bring about our desired outcome. As a famous quote attributed to psychoanalyst Carl Jung goes, "What you resist not only persists, but will grow in size." The opposite is often also true: When we push for something, such as someone entering recovery or choosing to be in a relationship with us, we actually push those things away.

Below I have outlined some reasons why learning to detach is a recommended practice for recovering from codependency.

YOU CAN'T CHANGE OTHERS

Trying to change people can backfire and lead to resentment—they will resent us, and we will resent them. It's important to understand that each person has the right to think and act according to their own system of values. Furthermore, we all have the right to make our own choices and make our own mistakes. But with this right comes the responsibility of dealing with the consequences of our choices. People make true changes only when they are ready, and their readiness must come from within—it can never be forced. It is painful to love someone who is struggling in ways you feel you can fix, but change must happen on that person's terms. We can only influence people to change if they are receptive, never more than that.

Early in my career, I felt compelled to "fix" my clients to prove my worth as their therapist and to release them from their suffering. This was a lot of pressure on myself but mostly on them, because when they inevitably did not do things "perfectly" (based on my flawed definition of what their healing should be), I took it personally. I wanted to be the best healer. This proved to be a trap for both therapist and client. I have since learned that I may guide or plant seeds but can take neither the responsibility nor the praise for someone's healing.

YOU CAN SOLVE ONLY SO MANY PROBLEMS

If we could all solve each other's problems, our world would be a very different place. The desire to take care of others would not be filled with so much pain, resentment, and guilt if we had the power to actually resolve others' issues. There are only some problems we truly have any power over solving, and these problems are our own or the ones we have co-created as adults (such as communication problems in a marriage). We are much more effective at solving a problem when it is our own problem. For example, I can alleviate the pain of my codependency by practicing mindfulness and detachment. I can never heal my codependency by fixing someone else; as we've learned, working to change someone is the hallmark of codependency itself. We are more productive and feel more empowered when we "stay in our own lane."

CARETAKING DOESN'T DEFINE YOU

Breaking out of codependency requires us to come to terms with accepting that we have inherent worth; we do not have to do anything to "earn" worth, and we cannot do anything that makes us truly worthless. Recovering from codependency is about respect and love for ourselves and others. Servitude is not loving to the self or to others, because the ultimate result of caretaking is resentment toward the person we are "caring" for. When I was growing up, my mother would frequently listen to "Ni Princesa, Ni Esclava," a song by Vicki Carr, about a woman who neither feels entitled to be a princess nor is a slave. She simply wants to give but also to receive in her relationships. Healthy relationships between adults truly are balanced in their giving and receiving.

YOUR WAY MAY NOT BE THE RIGHT WAY

Typically, our desire to change or control others comes from a sincerely loving place—we want to shield them from pain and suffering. However, we cannot always know the right path for another person. A person's choices, even if we view them as wrong, are a representation of their values, feelings of self, and free will. It is respectful to honor others' right to make their own choices and acknowledge their own responsibility in life—even if they aren't the best choices. In adult relationships, ideally, people respect one another's right to one's own views and to make one's own choices. Furthermore, in a healthy parent-child relationship, the parent teaches or guides the child, as developmentally appropriate, to care and think for himself or herself.

EXERCISE: Practicing Detachment

Detachment is not something we explicitly discuss with our loved ones; it is more an internal attitude of respect for self and other. We practice detachment when we hold back from giving advice, "saving" people from themselves, or forcing our agenda on someone. However, in our conversations with others, we can communicate in a way that clearly states authentically what we need or want while also validating that we do not have the right to force someone else into seeing things the same way we personally do. Below is a sample conversation between Carrie and her mother to explain this further:

MOTHER: I just don't understand what's wrong with you lately, Carrie. You have been so busy that you don't get to my house until 6 or 7 some nights. That is not enough time for me to be with you!

CARRIE: I'm really trying my best right now, Mom. I want to spend time with you, but work has been very demanding. I've let them know I need to be available for you, but they have given me a warning that if I leave early or call in anymore to be with you, I need to find another job. I can't afford to be out of work right now.

MOTHER: Can't you go in earlier? Don't you have money saved? I don't understand the problem. You used to be so much better at balancing everything in your life.

CARRIE: Mother, this is the best I can do right now—I understand that you do not see it that way.

Here, we can see Carrie communicating that although she values being with her mother, she must also maintain her job while also accepting that she cannot change her mother's perspective. She understands that trying to convince her mother of seeing things exactly the same way as she does will be a wasted effort, so she maintains her boundary of needing to have her job while also acknowledging that she is doing her best—even if her mother does not agree.

MINDFULNESS TIP

Learning how to detach takes mindful practice as well as validation of our fears alongside the importance of moving forward.

Restructuring Your Defenses

It is important to note that detachment is not dissociation, which can be defined as the opposite of mindfulness. Dissociation may represent as "spaciness," a refusal to look at the present, or forgetfulness. It can manifest when we are resisting the reality of what is actually happening because of a fantasy of what we wish were happening instead (our attachment to what we desire rather than accepting reality for what it is). When we dissociate, we deny what is happening in our lives or minimize the effects of trauma or other major events. Detachment, on the other hand, involves a mindful awareness of what truly is happening. Detachment is letting go of the outcome by being fully present.

Please read the section below; if it resonates with you, it may be useful to make an audio recording of it to listen to as needed or to journal a reflection about it.

Dear Me,

I'm really scared right now of letting go because this situation really matters to me. While I'm exhausted from trying to change and take care of others, I'm also scared that everything will fall apart without my efforts to control things. Nonetheless, I commit to learning to detach, and accept that detachment is a practice rather than a one-time decision. I am learning that I can focus on changing or controlling my response to others in the world, and I can cope with whatever comes my way. I promise to continue to work on discovering my inherent worth and value. Finally, I will work on honoring that I am a separate person from others; I have separate feelings, needs, wants, flaws, and strengths, and I will work on honoring others' separateness as well. They have a right to their own views, emotions, and needs. I am committed to practicing detachment because I am learning there is an alternative to how I live now; there can be less pain, stress, guilt, and anger. When I practice detachment, I see my life can be filled with more joy, peace, and connection.

Love, Me

TAKE IT FURTHER

In this chapter, we learned about family roles and how they contribute to codependency. Also highlighted was how these roles maintain homeostasis for a family rather than being authentic expressions of self. Hopefully, you learned more about your role(s) in the family as well as the ones your family members fit into. We understand that although these roles can be limiting and exhausting, it can be very scary to change. The practice of detachment was identified as a way to begin breaking free of these limitations and heal from codependency.

I ask you to contemplate the following:

1. Think about a person in your life around whom it feels safe to be authentic, like your brother or your best friend.

2. Consider what advice or guidance you would want to give your younger self when you were stuck in a certain role. What advice would you share now that you know you felt you had to be the Mascot, for example, or any other role?

3. Write a letter to your younger self with this advice and guidance. In this letter, you can also express your desire to help this child find his or her voice and authentic self.

Part Two
THE STEPS

Step 1
Get in Touch with Your "Self"

Caroline can't remember the last time she didn't feel exhausted, lonely, and miserable. She feels like her husband and children see her only as the chauffeur, chef, and maid. It's gotten so bad that Caroline no longer makes time to see her friends or work out, both of which she used to enjoy. Furthermore, while she used to enjoy sex, she now resents her husband when he initiates it because it just feels like another demand of her. She rarely has a moment to herself, but when she does, she notices an underlying panic that she no longer knows who she is outside of being a wife and mom. She doesn't like this feeling, so she avoids down time throughout the day. When she isn't busy doing things like preparing meals, planning parties, or attending soccer games, she posts to social media about these activities. She takes special care to ensure things look perfect and everyone looks happy in her posts. If someone likes or comments on her posts, she notices she feels a little less alone for a moment. Lately, to unwind at night, she has begun drinking more. She often posts cheerful pictures with captions like "Mommy's wine time." Sadly, these posts get lots of likes, which reinforces the cycle.

Who Are You?

Many people struggling with codependency feel like they have lost themselves or they never knew who they were in the first place. Although it's a common feeling, many people are embarrassed to reveal they don't know themselves. Of course, many codependents were not given the gift of self-exploration early in life. Instead they were expected to perform a role within their family, which prevents them from connecting with their authenticity.

We can never lose our authentic self, but it can be hidden from us under layers of stress, pain, obsessive thinking, anger, or trauma. Still, there is a clear pathway to connection, even if you have never discovered who you are. We have an innate wisdom in our body about who we are and what we value if we learn to become mindful. Expressions such as "follow your heart" or "trust your gut" highlight this truth. In the book *The Alchemist*, by Paulo Coelho, the main character asks why he should listen to his heart. In response, he is told, "Because you will never again be able to keep it quiet. Even if you pretend not to have heard what it tells you, it will always be there inside you, repeating to you what you're thinking about life and the world." No one in the world knows you better than yourself.

Connecting with our authentic self is fundamental for codependency recovery. When we don't know who we are, we may often feel that we don't like ourselves. Like Caroline, you might feel lost in life. But don't fret. Learning how to love yourself is a process. It begins with familiarizing yourself with who you are. We must know who we are to begin to like and respect ourselves, and then, in the practice of self-respect and self-care, we find that eventually, we have fallen in love with who we are.

In recovery, we are grounded in knowing who we authentically are, so we no longer live in reactivity. We become grounded in our sense of self-worth and the fact that we have options in how we respond and cope. Therefore, things may upset us, but like a tree, we stay rooted even if our branches sway on stormy days. In this way of living, we never forget our worthiness and sense of empowerment.

TAKE AN INVENTORY
(IDENTIFY NEGATIVE BEHAVIORAL PATTERNS)

It is important to look at the negative behavioral patterns in your life. Sometimes it can feel more manageable to make immediate changes to our behaviors than to our thoughts or beliefs. For example, while Caroline may not feel it's productive for her to practice self-care, she may notice that she's unable to do much after having a few drinks. She may also notice that drinking often leads to hangovers the next day, which impacts her mood and energy levels. Through this realization, she may realize she has time to take a bath and journal at night—and therefore prevent hangovers. Caroline can begin to replace drinking with healthy activities.

To build awareness of your own behaviors that harm you more than help you, you may want to look back at the Codependency Questionnaire (page 10) in chapter 1. In your journal, list 5 to 10 of these behaviors that strike you as the most problematic in your life currently. Identifying these behaviors may help you begin to see concrete ways you can begin to make changes. For each behavior, contemplate a way you can begin to change it; for example, you may agree with the statement, "It is common for me to say yes when I want to say no." If this is true, you can see that beginning to say no, or even saying "Let me think about it" when you need to, is a step toward respecting yourself.

It is important to take this inventory from a place of curiosity rather than from attacking yourself. Remember, you developed these behaviors as a reaction to painful experiences or messages in your life. You can have empathy for yourself and take steps toward change.

CLAIM YOUR WANTS AND NEEDS

Learning to identify and nurture our authentic needs and wants is a powerful step toward self-discovery. Human beings share common needs, those things essential for survival and health. Basic needs include food, safety, shelter, and sleep, and neglecting these needs comes at a high price to our mental and physical health. In order to more deeply know ourselves, we must first meet these basic needs. Maslow's hierarchy of needs highlights this fundamental truth; Maslow revealed that before we can ever have intimate relationships with others or feel whole and accomplished (self-actualization), we must have our basic needs met. Survival is the most basic drive for us as human beings, and if we aren't safe or if our physical needs aren't met, we don't have the mental or physical capacity to pursue a satisfied life based on authentic wants.

Wants, while not necessary for survival, add satisfaction and joy to our lives. We need shelter, but having a home that's nicely decorated and at the perfect temperature to our personal preference is a want. Additionally, we don't literally need pleasant ways to spend our time, but having enjoyable hobbies adds fun and peace to life. It is important to note that our persona—not our true self but, rather, an idea of who we *should* be—may be driven to various activities that do not meet our authentic desires. It is common to not know exactly what activities you enjoy, but it is important to give yourself permission to experiment to find what truly resonates with you. For example, your ego may tell you that the only hobbies that are truly valuable are ones like hiking or gardening because they are physically productive, but authentically, you may get the most joy from learning and reading. This is not only okay but worth celebrating! Your passions highlight who you truly are, and it's powerful to discover your essence.

RECONNECT WITH EARLY PASSIONS

Even if you grew up in a rigidly codependent family, it is common to have discovered your first passions in childhood and adolescence. Reconnecting with the activities you loved as a child or teenager can help you feel like you are coming back home to yourself. These activities may range from playing with a pet or playing board games to listening to music, drawing, or playing a sport. The emphasis here is to allow yourself to play—to have fun without needing to produce something. It allows us to reduce stress, encourages creativity, and promotes connection with the self and others.

Of course, it may be difficult to remember these first passions initially, as our true self can become hidden. Rediscovering these loved hobbies can be supported by looking at old photos or mementos from those earlier periods of our life. Sometimes just listening to music from when we were younger can help us remember who we are.

EXERCISE: Identifying Your Needs and Wants

To begin to identify your own needs and wants, please take time to journal about the following two prompts:

If no one else could judge me, what would I authentically want out of my life? Where would I want to live? What sort of education or work would I pursue? What sorts of relationships would I have?

How do I define a meaningful and successful life outside of others' definitions?

After journaling these responses, take a moment to reflect. Are any of these areas in your life already congruent with your authentic desires? If so, congratulations! This shows how capable you are of continuing this work. If not, now you have more information about what will allow you to feel satisfied in your life.

EXERCISE: Downward Arrow Technique

We can make behavioral changes after taking our inventory and identifying our needs and wants, but core beliefs will likely still influence us. In this exercise, we'll see how a stressful situation can help clarify which core beliefs are keeping us stuck.

To start, here's an example of Caroline's practice with this technique. She wrote,

> "I do all these things for my husband and kids, but they're never grateful. I ask them repeatedly to acknowledge all that I do and give up for them—friends, a social life, sleep— but they never do. They never help—my kids complain so much when I ask for help that I've just stopped. It's not worth the fight. And after years of begging to be treated with respect from my husband, I've given up."

If this is true, what does that mean?
Since no one ever helps out, it means I'm not appreciated.

If this is true, what does that mean?
If I'm not appreciated, then all the things I work so hard to do for them don't matter.

If this is true, what does that mean?
If the things I do don't matter, then I don't matter; I'm useless and invisible.

"I don't matter; I'm useless and invisible" is the core negative belief.

In your journal, try this for yourself. Identify a situation in which you feel resentment or stress, and then continue to ask yourself, "If this is true, what does that mean?" Keep going until you identify a core belief. You'll have a good sense when you've arrived at this belief—you will just know it or feel it. Later on, we'll work on how you can address and change this core belief.

Create a New Narrative

We tell ourselves stories to help us make sense of what we experience. Although these narratives are created by our own perceptions, they can begin to feel like the absolute truth. Typically, they center on our core beliefs. Then, we look for

proof that reinforces these beliefs and discard anything to
the contrary. People who see themselves as weak will be sure
to remember times they sacrificed what they needed but will
overlook times that reflect their strength, such as when they
successfully negotiated for a promotion at work.

THE STORIES WE TELL

It is human nature to create stories based on our personal experiences so that our lives feel cohesive and organized. Unfortunately,
the narrative we create can be self-destructive, as we often build
it around our negative beliefs. For example, Caroline believes she
exists to serve others. She created this idea of herself at age eight,
when her mother became paraplegic after a car accident. Her
mother became stuck in her grief and refused to seek support.
She would often isolate herself in bed. Caroline realized that she
was now responsible to care for everyone. She learned to cook for
the family and made sure her sisters were dressed for school every
day and were put to bed at night. Since then, she has believed she
is useless if she's not serving someone else.

SEPARATING THE SELF

In our storytelling, we tie our identity to our problems. If we
are struggling with codependency, it's not uncommon to feel
broken. It is important to understand that you are not the
problem. You are a person with a complex history and reasons
for struggling to value your internal self-worth and reality, but
this is not the essence of who you are. You have codependency,
but codependency does not define you. When you notice codependency does not embody your authentic self, you can begin
to fight the problem rather than attack yourself.

We can use our creativity to externalize problems. When
I was struggling with depression, one day I had an epiphany.

I was not a broken and unlovable person, but my depression was trying to convince me that I was. In my mind, depression looked like a giant cockroach with a crown. After externalizing her, when I had depressed thoughts, I could notice that the roach was a liar. Can you think of a totem or representation of codependency that you can use in a similar fashion?

CHANGING YOUR PERSPECTIVE

Over time, after noticing the cockroach, I tapped into a realization about myself that my depression never let me see: I am very strong for surviving abuse in my childhood. I realized this strength is authentic, and when I embody this truth, I am a goddess warrior. When we externalize the problem, it allows room to see the parts of us we have neglected to notice. For example, Caroline believes she does not matter if she is not doing things for others, but she can change the story by noticing other perspectives. She may remember that when her children were babies, they literally could do nothing for others but were inherently valuable. This can allow her to see her inherent worth without needing to do anything, too.

DECONSTRUCT TO RECONSTRUCT

The stories we tell ourselves can be used as a form of support, or we can use them to tear ourselves down. Despite the fact that there are numerous interpretations available to us, many of us are attached to a specific narrative of our lives, such as believing we are always invisible to others and therefore worthless, or believing that no matter what, we are rejected and abandoned by others. Luckily, we can learn how to challenge our painful—and often victimized—narratives. We can do this by deconstructing our stories. To do so, we tell the story of what happened, but we don't stop there; now we begin to notice events we often dismiss that challenge our original narrative. For instance, you may feel invisible because your parents were neglectful, but you might then notice that while you were growing up, your best friend's parents took a great interest in you, so, you see, you cannot be inherently invisible.

In Caroline's case, she may tell the story of her childhood, but as she goes through her timeline, she may remember her aunt came to live with her family for a few years when she was 10. She may notice that her aunt was supportive and encouraged her to spend time with friends. Caroline may also notice that she declined this encouragement because she felt obligated to be home. This challenges Caroline's story of being worthless if she wasn't doing for others. She can then continue to challenge her story by noticing other times she was accepted just for being her. She will also see that at times, she was the one neglecting herself.

EXERCISE: Write Your Story

Please set aside some quiet time to journal about how you believe you developed codependency, and reflect on how your core belief from the Downward Arrow Technique (page 51) ties into this story. Think about your core belief and experiences in your life that reinforced this belief. Next, notice times in your life that challenge your core belief. Situations that contradict your narrative highlight that there is another way of seeing yourself and your life outside your original narrative. Once you have noticed the times that contradict your original narrative, set some time aside to journal about what you are discovering about who you really are. Rather than what your narrative has told you, what are you now seeing is true? How does it feel to notice what's true about you in a way that challenges the original belief? How can you behave or act differently now that you see the truth?

For example, you may think about how your childhood contributed to believing others know your truth or reality much better than you. Perhaps your parents often claimed you were wrong when you commented on situations, such as telling you that you didn't see your father slap your mother when you *know* you did. This created a narrative that your perception of reality is wrong, even when it comes to your own perspective. You may also notice other scenarios that reinforced this belief, such as how your college boyfriend said you were paranoid by thinking he was cheating on you. Next, begin to acknowledge times that challenge your narrative of being unable to trust yourself. You may remember that when you were young, you heard a quiet voice inside you say that becoming a teacher would be the right career for you, so you pursued this. You are now very happy in your career, so you were *right* in this choice. Or, you may see that when you were told you were paranoid by your college boyfriend, you later discovered he was in fact cheating on you, so you had been *correct*. You can now see that you are able to trust the way you perceive things, because you have been accurate in the past. You can begin to trust listening to yourself more now, because you now know your original narrative was not true.

Releasing Shame

Brené Brown, a professor who has done a lot of research on the topic of shame, defines shame as "the intensely painful feeling or experience of believing that we are flawed and therefore unworthy of love and belonging." It can be embarrassing to acknowledge how we have enabled, accepted, or allowed hurtful behaviors and neglected ourselves in our codependency. Recovering from code-pendency requires the ability to release shame.

Many of us try to fight shame with shame. Like a harsh and critical parent, we may tell ourselves what a mess we are and that we need to get it together. However, fighting shame with shame is like trying to fight a fire with gasoline—it only fuels our pain. The antidote to shame is self-compassion. There are reasons for our behaviors, even as we are still accountable. Let's talk about how to release shame.

LETTING GO OF SHAME-BASED BELIEFS

Shame tells us we are not good enough as our imperfect self. It drives us to strive for perfection and to please others in order to be accepted and prove our worth. Shame tells us impossible things, such as "I must be accepted by everyone" or "I cannot make mistakes." Of course, these shame-based beliefs are impossible to live up to and lead to anxiety and misery. Furthermore, allowing shame to dictate our life disconnects us from our authentic self and others. The sad irony of working to be accepted by all is that we are actually keeping away the richest, most intimate relationships possible, because there are some people in this world who will celebrate us in all our authentic glory, while we may be incompatible with others.

DON'T AVOID DISCOMFORT

As a result of codependency, you have already survived a lot of pain, anger, and anxiety. I'm bringing this up only because it means you can certainly tolerate some discomfort. While working through your recovery, remember that the rewards are worth it. A traditional narrative suggests that we gain maturity simply as a by-product of aging. This isn't true for all. There are many people who reach a ripe old age but never actually mature. They never discovered their authentic self. They never found a way to maintain a joyful and satisfying life. As the spiritual teacher Marianne Williamson wrote, "It takes courage . . . to endure the sharp pains of self-discovery rather than choose to take the dull pain of unconsciousness that would last the rest of our lives."

IT'S NOT YOUR FAULT

Finally, I want you to remember that there are reasons you thought your value in this world is conditional. Therefore, there are reasons you have behaved the way you have and believed what you have in your codependency. You didn't know there was an alternative before, but now that you do, you are doing the beautiful and mature work of taking responsibility for your healing.

EXERCISE: Can You Accept It?

When we begin to do our recovery work and look at our histories and narratives, it can be common to feel new waves of anger toward those we feel set us up for codependency. We may also feel shame. Consider that indulging these feelings doesn't lead to recovery. Instead, we heal by coming to terms with and accepting what was a part of our life.

For this exercise, think about something in your past that you are feeling resentful toward or damaged by. Take a moment to journal about this. You do not have to be happy about this past event. You need simply to accept that it is true and part of your history.

Although it may have been upsetting and painful, what happened to you does not define you. Journal about how your life, mood, or beliefs may change if you allow yourself to fully accept the past. Also, please note that accepting the past doesn't equal forgiveness.

Identify Your Internal Beliefs

In Breaking Unhelpful Thought Patterns (page 34), we worked on identifying some unhelpful thoughts, and in this first step, we have further clarified how to identify our core belief systems. Negative core beliefs limit our understanding—and appreciation—of ourselves, as well as limit how close we can become to others in an interdependent way. Identifying our beliefs is a valuable step toward recovery, because we can then work on challenging these beliefs so we can feel more confident and whole.

THE PROCESS

We all have an inner critic. For some of us, that critic is quite loud. Your inner critic may tell you that you're weak, stupid, or disgusting. You may want to look back on your journal entry about your unhelpful thoughts, as these will clarify your negative beliefs, as well. Finally, you can use the Downward Arrow Technique (page 51) for multiple situations to clarify your beliefs.

CORE BELIEFS ARE MISTAKEN FOR VALUE JUDGMENTS

The thoughts and stories we have about ourselves often overlook the exceptions that would contradict this negative self-view. In therapy, we like to say a belief is simply a thought you think often. However, thinking something frequently doesn't make it an absolute truth.

REPLACING CORE BELIEFS

Many of my clients say even though they have been told to affirm themselves—by saying "I love myself" or "I'm worthy of love and respect," for example—they still hate themselves and view themselves as innately unworthy or somehow broken. They feel more shame because they cannot affirm their worth. To replace our negative core beliefs, we must do two things: First, continue to look for the sparkling events that challenge our narrative or belief system. For example, if Caroline wants to challenge the belief that she's unappreciated and unimportant, she will intentionally look out for times when her family members or others give her a genuine thank-you or offer assistance. The next step for replacing core beliefs is outlined in the following exercise: Identifying and Replacing Negative Core Beliefs.

EXERCISE: Identifying and Replacing Negative Core Beliefs

Many of us are already familiar with the concept of positive affirmation to replace negative self-talk, but I understand this process as a bridge. While our eventual goal may be to fully believe the statement "I love myself," we start incrementally. What's a small way we can challenge our negative beliefs? To use myself as an example, in my early 20s I didn't like myself. I felt invisible. The idea of claiming to love myself felt offensive, as I believed it was fundamentally untrue. I started with something more simple: "I exist." I would stare into the mirror to reinforce this. From there, I was able to say, "I want to like myself" and "I'm working on loving myself." Finally, after taking this measured and honest approach, I now can say "I love myself" with ease.

For this exercise, identify a negative core belief that interferes with your self-view and relationships. Identify what you would ultimately like to believe: for example, "I don't have to be perfect to be happy" or "I can be happy and accept myself as I am." Then identify two or three bridge affirmations, such as "I am learning to accept that I have strengths and flaws but am still worthwhile" or "My life can still be joyful even when I make mistakes, because mistakes are a part of life."

Caroline can use this bridge technique to replace her negative core beliefs. One of her core beliefs is "I don't matter; I'm useless and invisible." At this early stage, she may not yet be ready to affirm, "I matter just because I exist; I have inherent worth." However, she is more comfortable affirming, "Human beings are born worthwhile just for being. I'm beginning to notice the same is true for me." After this feels true to her, she can then affirm, "I was born inherently worthy and continue to be." This statement is much closer to the goal affirmation but still provides some distance, as it helps her understand she was worthy from birth but doesn't say she is worthy outright. It's a small difference, but semantics can help her believe the truth of her worth. Finally, she can then affirm, "I matter just because I exist. I have inherent worth."

Letting Go of the "Victim" Mentality

Due to the external focus that codependency encourages, it's common to feel that someone else, or even life itself, is victimizing us. We can feel helpless, like a plastic bag in the wind. But as we recover, we learn we are never truly stuck or helpless. We have options regarding our choices, actions, and responses.

Acknowledging our responsibility for our personal behaviors and the relationships we engage in can be a challenge. This may be hard to accept, but codependency doesn't mean you are a victim. People may have treated us terribly, but we also choose to co-create and continue those patterns. We make the choice to deny or minimize the behavior of others, and we choose to neglect our own needs and ourselves.

When we feel victimized, we forget our power. When we're attached to feeling like a victim, we forget we can change. It's within our power to acknowledge the pain and anger we hold toward others and release it. We become stuck when we refuse to accept that we can't change our past; we can only come to terms with it. It is liberating to remember, however, that we do have the power to change our lives in the present and the future.

TAKE IT FURTHER

In this step, we identified how common it is to feel lost in codependency, and we looked at ways to connect with our authentic self. Narratives and negative belief systems were discussed as barriers to seeing the truth of our wholeness and worthiness. To continue the work outlined in this step, please do the following:

1. Repeat your "bridge" affirmation at least once daily; it can help to put up a Post-it somewhere you will frequently see it, such as your bathroom mirror. Looking in the mirror while you say this affirmation can help build self-compassion, too, as you have likely been much more critical of yourself than of others, and looking at yourself can help reduce this.

2. Dita Von Teese said, "You can be a delicious, ripe peach and there will still be people in the world that hate peaches." Journal about how you feel about pleasing people and being accepted by others in general and what feelings come up as you reflect on this quote.

3. In this step, you were able to start noticing a new narrative of yourself—moving from weak to strong, for example. If you were able to identify a character or totem that represents your new narrative, find a picture of it and use it as your phone or computer wallpaper, or, if not, choose an inspirational quote that highlights this new self-view and put it in a place you look often, as a way to reinforce the message.

Step 2
Prioritize Self-Care

Oscar and Cassandra have been married for 15 years and dated for 3 years before that. Prior to getting married, their relationship felt easy. All their friends talked about how perfect they were together. Oscar took all these things as a sign that Cassandra was "the one," and proposed. They never discussed their vision for the future. Oscar assumed everything would fall into place when he met the right person. A few years after getting married, Oscar started talking about having a family, which had always been important to him. Cassandra shared that she didn't know this was important to him and that she needed more time to achieve goals at work before considering motherhood. Oscar accepted this and waited until Cassandra got to a good place with her career before he brought it up again. And Cassandra again said it wasn't the right time. With a sinking sensation in his stomach, Oscar went along with it. In fact, he had started working longer hours, and if he came home late, Cassandra would be asleep and therefore unable to continue their discussions about having kids. This went on for years, causing Oscar to feel resentful. He saw his colleagues with families and wondered how his wife could deny something so important to him. However, he loved her and didn't want to leave, so when these feelings came up, he put them to the side. These days, he's noticed that treating himself to leftovers in the office kitchen in the afternoons helps him feel better. Oscar has started to feel depressed with the weight he is gaining, but he feels emotionally drained, so he continues to overeat to deal with these uncomfortable feelings.

This Is Your Time

Early in your recovery from codependency is the time for you to shift your focus from someone else to yourself. Of course, this very act is revolutionary and challenging. When we begin to change, it is very natural to want to have the person we are in a codependent relationship with to change with us. While that would be ideal, the very nature of codependent relationships may make this not possible, at least in the beginning.

WHEN THEY DON'T UNDERSTAND

In a codependent relationship, it can be difficult when one party is committed to making changes and the other person is not. They may have reasons for refusing to join you on this journey. It's possible that the other person in the relationship doesn't feel motivated to change because they don't recognize there is a problem. The other person may feel accepting of the dynamics between the two of you even if they are dissatisfying to you. Cassandra may not realize there are issues in her marriage with Oscar because when they talk about kids, she believes he gets confused sometimes but agrees truthfully that he is happy not having children.

WHEN THEY WON'T SUPPORT YOU

Sometimes it's not that the other person can't understand your needs; it's that they won't support your efforts to change. The person you're in a codependent relationship with may not realize it is the cycle of the relationship itself that's the problem. We discussed the narrative of the victim in the previous step, and for many of us, it is much easier to look outside of ourselves to identify why we are unhappy. The other person in the relationship may be scapegoating you, unfortunately, as the problem. They may feel that if only you were less needy or sensitive, then everything would be smooth sailing between the two of you. This is unfair. In any relationship, homeostasis requires both people to maintain it. In other words, your partner plays an equal role in whatever they perceive as "not working" in your relationship. But even if you are being scapegoated, it is still true that you are responsible to care for yourself, and you can break out of homeostasis by focusing on your own change.

YOU CAN'T CHANGE THEM

It can be painful to not have your partner be willing to change with you; it may even trigger some of your negative, shame-based beliefs. However, their unwillingness to change is not about your worth. Rather, it highlights the very nature of codependent relationships. Your partner has reasons for being at peace with the situation or simply doesn't feel the need to change. It's necessary to restate that this is not about your fundamental worth. Practice detachment and remind yourself that you can't change anyone. You may have future hopes that you both recover, but it's essential that you continue on your journey of self-care and healing. This is the true path out of codependency.

DEALING WITH LONELINESS

It may feel lonely to not have the person you feel closest to alongside you in your recovery. Nonetheless, support is still available to you. As you heal, it is important to focus on self-care, but interdependent people also accept support. This will be discussed later in this step.

EXERCISE: Identifying Unhealthy Coping Strategies

In this exercise, identify from this list some of your possible unhealthy coping strategies. Also, if any other harmful behavior you engage in is not listed here, please write it down in your journal. Then reflect on the following: Do any of these statements stand out to you? Think about the negative consequences of this coping behavior. Are you willing to replace it?

- I go over my budget to reward myself if I've had a hard week.

- I binge-eat snacks, such as chips or cookies, after a long day.

- I keep my worries to myself and hide out in my house all weekend if stressed.

- I have cut or burned myself to deal with my pain/stress/anger.

- I tell people what I really think of them and get in verbal and/or physical fights.

- I am worried that I may watch too much pornography and/or masturbate too often.

- I have cheated on my partner to feel better and/or get back at them.

- I often unwind by using alcohol or drugs.

- I don't take my medications as prescribed.

- I restrict my food or obsessively count calories to feel "in control."

- I engage in illegal behaviors, such as shoplifting, public sex, or vandalizing.

- I often have road rage and scream at other drivers from my car.

- I sleep excessively to "check out."

- I gamble money that I cannot afford to lose.

- I drink caffeine excessively rather than get enough sleep.

- I miss out on social events with friends or family to work long hours or give up my paid vacation time.

> Self-care is not a justification for self-harming or engaging in unhealthy behaviors. Self-care is the practice to which we can connect with self-love. If we truly love ourselves, we will not abuse and neglect ourselves. Self-care allows us to cope with life in a loving and respectful way. We begin to care for our mental, physical, and social health, like a nurturing parent.

Get Serious about Self-Care

Self-care can be challenging early in recovery, as self-neglect is a hallmark of codependency. But allow me to pay you a compliment: You have already begun your self-care practice by picking up this book! In recovery, the way we build strong roots is with self-care. Learning how to practice self-care can be overwhelming, so I think it's useful to begin with the fundamentals: sleep, food, exercise, and routine medical care. I attribute at least half of my recovery to a consistent focus on diet and exercise, which shifted my mood immediately. This positive effect allowed me to think more clearly and take the steps I needed to change my behaviors and relationships. What's interesting is that our gut is known to be our "second brain" for a variety of reasons, an important one being that 95 percent of the body's serotonin is found in the bowels. Serotonin is a neurotransmitter that helps to regulate mood, sleep, sexual desire, and memory. Depression has been linked to low serotonin levels. Eating a diet rich in fruits and vegetables along with whole grains and fermented foods has been shown to keep the gut healthy. All I ask is that you try your best caring for yourself. You don't have to be a gym rat or a health nut; you just have to be open to living a life with more self-care.

YOU ARE WORTHY

Self-care is not selfish or indulgent. Rather, it is the practice of honoring the natural rhythms of life—there are times to plant and times to harvest. Living in a balanced and satisfying way requires us to respect that rest and play are as crucial as producing. Without self-care, our bodies will break down. It is common for codependents to exhaust themselves to the point of frequent illness, immune issues, or headaches from self-neglect. After all, we can drive a brand-new car for a couple years, but without any routine maintenance, eventually it will break down to the point that it may be more cost-effective to replace it. We don't have the option to trade in our body, so the way we treat it can lead to positive or negative consequences. You deserve mental, emotional, and physical health; therefore, you deserve self-care.

WHAT DO YOU ENJOY?

A major barrier to self-care is being unaware of what nourishes us or brings us joy. Self-care is nourishment for our whole self. We feed our social self by connecting with community. We nurture our mind through practices like therapy or medication, if needed, but also through learning and allowing creativity. If the spiritual self is important, we practice self-care by going to church or participating in a community of like-minded individuals.

Initially, we may need to allow time to discover what we enjoy. After all, with consideration, most of us have passions outside our work, such as cooking, music, or gardening. Think about the little extras in life that bring you a sense of happiness, such as the sound of a wind chime on your porch, a beautiful painting over your bed, or scented candles. Begin to integrate these things into your daily living for ongoing nourishment.

PRACTICE GRATITUDE

It's common to fixate on what's not working in our lives, but in recovery, we learn to shift our focus to what's already good. The things in our lives that are good help us see that we have reasons to be grateful *now*. Numerous studies have found that focusing on gratitude improves happiness, reduces stress, and allows us to feel more satisfied with our relationships.

I kept a gratitude journal for a few months. Every morning, I listed three things for which I felt grateful. I began to notice the good in my life, like someone letting me merge when there was bad traffic or a kind stranger cheerfully smiling and greeting me. I noticed how uplifting these things felt when I saw the kind energy of what was being given to me. Of course, we have a running list of what we appreciate, such as family and friends, but rather than list these things automatically, try tapping into the emotional energy of our appreciation. This exercise pushed me to be creative.

EXERCISE: Self-Care Schedule

Self-care is an ongoing goal in recovery. It may seem intimidating, but with enough practice, self-care becomes natural and integrated into your daily life. The way I structure my life now is dramatically different than prior to my recovery, where my day might consist of work, TV, surfing the web, and talking to a friend about all my complaints. What follows is a sample schedule for my life today:

- Wake with enough time to not have to rush to work. Have a little treat to look forward to such as my fresh coffee from beans I grind each morning.

- Prepare or pick up a healthy lunch for myself. I have learned that if I indulge in fried or sugary foods, it becomes difficult for me to do work in the afternoons as they drain my energy, which makes me irritable.

- Listen to an entertaining podcast during my commute.

- Get to work and center myself by outlining my tasks for the day.

- Make sure to take a midday break, even if it's just 20 minutes. I need this time to recharge—if the weather allows, I also walk around my office building for a bit to help clear my thoughts.

- After finishing work at the end of the work day, drive home and call my best friend.

- Do some gentle yoga prior to dinner.

Mindfulness: How It Helps

One of the best ways to begin to cultivate joy and practice self-care is to learn to be mindful of the positives that come our way. They can be as small as drinking an excellent cup of coffee, listening to an interesting podcast on our commute, watching the tree we planted start to produce fruit, taking a walk after dinner with our children, or browsing a bookstore. When your attention moves to ruminating about something you don't like or that you want to change, move your focus to the present moment while being curious. Sometimes, we must challenge ourselves to look for the good in any given moment. For example, we may be stuck in a boring meeting, but we may also notice that we are wearing our most comfortable work outfit, and we can pay attention to how soft the fabric feels against our skin. Continuing to move your focus to the present moment while learning how to notice what is good can significantly improve your perspective and mood.

- Take zinc, a probiotic, and melatonin (if needed).
- Give myself a foot massage.
- Rub lavender oil on my wrists.
- Watch an autonomous sensory meridian response (ASMR) video or do a guided meditation.
- Go to bed early enough to allow for a full night of sleep.

For this exercise, think of a typical day with its typical demands, such as work or childcare, and begin to contemplate the areas in which you already do things that you look forward to. For example, maybe you often get to chat with a friend while the two of you wait at your children's school to pick them up, or you always make sure to attend your monthly book club. Furthermore, remember that this exercise is about integrating small pleasures to relax and enjoy life. Think about where you want to start, like getting more exercise or sleep, and consider ways to integrate these activities by making notes about them in your journal. Outline a schedule that feels realistic to you while taking into account self-care.

EXERCISE: Observing Emotions

Emotions provide information about where we are in any given moment. There are no bad emotions. However, there are uncomfortable and comfortable feelings. Even before we know what we are feeling, whether it's pleasant or unpleasant, our emotions originate in the body. Expressions such as "That really gets on my nerves" or "I felt my blood boil" highlight this truth.

Learning to tune into the physical sensations of our emotions is highly informative. This exercise will demonstrate that emotions, when we allow them to do so, move up and out of us. We are responsible for honoring them rather than stifling them. For example, think of a time you cried. In the middle of it, you may have felt your pain would go on forever, but after some time, you started to breathe more deeply again and felt some relief.

In your journal, make some notes on the following:

THINK ABOUT A TIME YOU FELT ANGER. Think about the situation, who was there, and what was happening. Take a deep breath and notice what your body and breath are doing at this time—maybe you are holding your breath or clenching your fist. Take note of how anger feels in your body.

THINK ABOUT A TIME YOU FELT GUILTY. Think about the situation, who was there, and what was happening. Take a deep breath and notice what your body and breath are doing now. Perhaps you may notice changes in your belly. Take note of how guilt feels in your body.

THINK ABOUT A TIME YOU FELT FEAR OR ANXIETY. Think about the situation, who was there, and what was happening. Take a deep breath and notice what your body and breath are doing, and pay special attention to your chest. Take note of how fear or anxiety feels in your body.

THINK ABOUT A TIME YOU FELT ASHAMED OR EMBARRASSED. Think about the situation, who was there, and what was happening. Take a deep breath and notice what your body and breath are doing, and pay special attention to your belly. Take note of how shame feels in your body.

THINK ABOUT A TIME YOU FELT LOVE. Think about the situation, who was there, and what was happening. Take a deep breath and notice what your body and breath are doing. Take note of the sensations attached to your feeling of love.

THINK ABOUT A TIME YOU FELT JOY. Think about the situation, who was there, and what was happening. Take a deep breath and notice what your body and breath are doing. Take note of what joy feels like for you.

You may not notice your physical sensations for all the emotions initially. Don't worry, that's okay! Just practice tuning in when you are feeling something—notice what your body is doing, as it will help you know more quickly what you are feeling and what you need, and may highlight that you need to practice self-care.

Getting Support

As we discussed, the other person in your codependent relationship may not be motivated to change. It's common to feel like a burden, and it takes incredible courage to reach out for support. We're not meant to live in isolation. There's no shame in asking for help. One person is not meant to plant the wheat, harvest it, grind the flour, bake the bread, and prepare the meals. Accepting support is fundamental to keeping ourselves healthy.

FAMILY AND FRIENDS
If there's anyone in your life you trust, consider sharing your recovery intentions with them. Doing so may be intimidating at first, but practice turning to them when you are feeling the need for support. Part of self-care is knowing when you need support and then asking for it.

WORKING WITH A THERAPIST
A therapist can be an amazing ally. You and your therapist will develop a plan to best guide your recovery. Some people have

negative feelings about therapy due to unfortunate previous experiences. I encourage you to try again if it's an affordable option. It may take a few tries to find the right therapist for you, but when it happens, it can be powerful and life changing.

12–STEP MEETINGS

There are numerous 12-step communities to help people struggling with particular issues. Some are familiar, such as Al-Anon, CODA, or SLAA, but there are meetings for those with unhealthy coping strategies as well, such as overeating, gambling, and working too much. In a 12-step community, not only do you have the anonymous support of those who can relate to you intimately, but you also have the opportunity to find a sponsor—someone who has done their 12-step recovery work and now, as part of their recovery, gives back by guiding someone else through their recovery process. This relationship has been incredibly nourishing for many. Of course, attendance at meetings is completely optional, as the 12-step philosophy doesn't resonate with everyone. This is completely okay—the goal in your recovery is to find the care that personally meets your needs.

YOU ARE PART OF YOUR SUPPORT TEAM!

Focusing on the positive is as much a part of self-care as engaging in fulfilling activities. Remind yourself that you have done your part. When I get stuck feeling that I need to do more, I think about the movie *Babe* and how the farmer would tell the pig at times, "That'll do, pig; that'll do." The same is true for each of us. Remember, we cannot do things perfectly in life or in recovery, so celebrating each success is the positive, mindful way.

EXERCISE: Who Can You Turn to?

Ideally, we have at least two or three people we can turn to when we need support. Not all of us have friends or family we feel we can trust, though. That's okay—remember we can get support in other settings. For this exercise, identify at least two people in your life that you can tell about your recovery process. Identify any thoughts or beliefs that may prevent you from reaching out to them while identifying the positive potential consequences of talking to them. If you cannot identify anyone, please consider seeking a sponsor or therapist. You may want to weigh the pros and cons of doing so, as you may feel anxious about it. This is totally normal, but remember that in recovery, we are working toward interdependence, which means seeking support.

TAKE IT FURTHER

In this step, we discussed the importance of a self-care practice as we recover from codependency to improve and maintain our mental and physical health. Nurturing ourselves allows us to move toward self-love. Developing a self-care practice will take time and commitment, but it is necessary to continue this work.

1. At this point, it is common to still feel uncertain about the value of self-care. If this is true for you, reflect on what negative consequences you, your work, and your loved ones may experience 5 or 10 years from now if you continue to put off self-care. Weigh the pros and cons of not changing versus the pros and cons of practicing self-care. Notice your values, as well, and how self-care supports them. For example, if you value time with family, you may notice that refusing to care for yourself now may eventually limit your time with grandchildren if you develop chronic health conditions.

2. When we value others more than our own self, it's common to neglect or even abuse ourselves with certain behaviors that we say help us destress. Take steps to reduce these behaviors in your life—often, this is easier when we replace the behavior with a new, healthier one. For example, if you tend to go home after a long day and shop online for items that you cannot afford (leading to more stress), perhaps you can take a hot bath instead. Every time you don't engage in a harmful behavior and choose a healthier one, you are one step closer to truly caring for yourself. Total abstinence from the behavior you want to replace is not necessary; rather, choosing self-care more often than self-neglect is the goal.

3. Reflect on your self-care schedule and how realistic it is for you at this time. In recovery, we practice daily self-care, but it does not need to be extreme to "count." Even the choice to take a few deep breaths before you make dinner for your family, or stretching after a work meeting, is progress. All that is necessary is consistent, but simple, efforts toward self-care.

Step 3
Build Boundaries

At 43, Lori cannot understand why, even though she has been able to achieve success professionally and has built an amazing community of friends and family, she has never been able to find a long-term healthy relationship. Her friends tell her she is attractive, kind, and fun. Although she dates, she has never found lasting commitment. Lori is convinced that she attracts only unavailable men and is skeptical there is even such a thing as an available and interesting man with whom she could feel mutual passion and love. Due to this skepticism, while she feels she truly wants commitment, she often recycles old boyfriends who have hurt her in the past. When they reconcile, she always protests to them that this is their last chance. She identifies as a hopeless romantic and really believes people can change. Therefore, prior to communicating about her limits and needs, she sleeps with them. She then feels more regret over this choice when, again, they are unwilling to commit to the relationship. After some time of being casual with them, she walks away due to the pain. She says she will not do this ever again, but when she feels lonely, the cycle repeats.

What Do You Want?

Establishing healthy boundaries allows us to fundamentally transform our lives. I liken boundaries to the fence around a house. This fence allows others in but also protects us from harmful words, behaviors, and expectations. We care about others, but we also honor what works for us. In codependency, we live in a state of extremes when it comes to boundaries. At times, you may have no boundaries and feel like others are walking all over you. When the pain of this becomes too much, you may emotionally disconnect from others altogether. Without healthy boundaries, we abandon ourselves, which can lead to self-loathing or losing a sense of who we are. Healthy boundaries allow us to protect ourselves so we can feel self-respect and self-love, just like a fence protects a house without completely shutting others out.

WHAT BOTHERS YOU?

Prior to asserting our boundaries, we must first identify what they are. When you begin this work, pay attention to your words and emotions. If you feel resentful or find yourself saying things like "I can't stand it" or "I can't believe you keep doing this to me," you've identified a personal boundary. Additionally, as discussed in step 2, Prioritize Self-Care (page 64), building mindfulness of your physical sensations can be very informative. When interacting with others, your body will give you clues as to what works for you and what doesn't. For example, if your stomach drops or your chest tightens when the person you just started dating says they only want something casual, this is a clear sign the arrangement does not meet your needs. However, if your body stays relaxed and open when others share their expectations, then you will know the situation aligns with what feels good for you, too. Building awareness of your own truth is an ongoing practice, and you can use the following exercise to guide you.

Set aside some time to be alone, and write down a list of beliefs in your journal. On this list, include statements that you know are true for you, as well as some you know are not true but that others expect of you, such as "I believe in God," "I value being a parent," or "It's important to have children." On this list, also include some beliefs you have picked up from your family or culture, such as "Mistakes are unacceptable" or "Pursuing the highest-paying job is more important than pursuing my passion." Next, put the list aside and begin to visualize your boundary. You may choose to make an audio recording of the following to help guide you:

Close your eyes and imagine you have a marker in any color you like. Begin to draw a circle around yourself with this marker and imagine this circle begins to grow up around you in the form of light. Breathe deeply as you allow this light to form a bubble all the way around you. In this bubble, you decide what is true for you and what is not. Now, read your statements and notice your body's reaction. If a statement resonates as true, reach out your hand and pull that statement into your bubble. If it's not true for you, then extend your arm in a *stop* gesture and say aloud, "That's not true" or "That does not fit" to keep the statement out.

Take some time to journal about what you noticed about yourself. How does it feel to imagine this bubble around you at all times, protecting you from others' words and expectations so that you can see if it meets your needs, too, prior to reacting?

Some people initially struggle to visualize their bubble. Just noticing that we can be protected in this way is a big, and sometimes scary, step toward recovery. If you are having a hard time seeing your bubble around you, reflect and journal on the following:

1. What messages did you receive growing up about people who do or don't set limits? These messages are sometimes spoken, such as when a mother complains about her sister being "selfish" if her sister turned down an invitation to a family event. They may also be unspoken, like having a father who never says no. What did that tell you?

2. Reflect back on the core beliefs you identified using the Downward Arrow Technique (page 51). Could any of these be preventing you from forming a boundary? For example, if you believe you can't depend on yourself, it will likely be scary to begin to set a healthy boundary that separates you from others, which is necessary to become interdependent.

3. Does self-protection feel like isolation? What do you need to trust yourself or feel comforted as you learn to self-protect? From this response, try developing a mantra for yourself, such as "It's an act of love for myself and others when I self-protect, because we can then have a healthy relationship."

Continue to work on this visualization. It can be done anywhere, whether waiting in line at the grocery store or in the comfort of your own home. Also, repeat your mantra. It may take practice—in codependency, we have a lot of experience being unprotected, so just being honest and patient with yourself as you develop your bubble is a major step toward recovery.

IT'S OKAY TO SET BOUNDARIES

People with healthy boundaries know they bring gifts to their relationships just by being who they naturally are. The foundation of their relationships is not duty, obligation, or desperation. They trust with certainty that there are people in this world who value them enough to respect their limits. Of course, early in recovery, it is common to feel like setting limits with others is unkind or mean. But respecting boundaries is the most loving thing we can do. After all, it's honest and prevents building unfair resentment toward others.

Types of Boundaries

I will outline some basic types of boundaries in this section. There may be some values we all agree with, like the need for physical safety, but overall, boundaries are unique to each person. This is because boundaries reflect our personal values and perspectives of truth. Our boundaries may be flexible, as they can be dependent on the relationship or how we are feeling. Your father may be allowed to give you a hug, but you may be uncomfortable with a hug from your supervisor. Or maybe you usually want to tell your best friend everything, but you feel tired and irritable one night, so you take a rain check on your scheduled call. In codependency, we often deny our boundaries and, therefore, disrespect ourselves. It is important to begin to consistently respect your personal limits, whatever they are.

MATERIAL

Material boundaries are about how you feel about others using, touching, or exploring your personal possessions and how you value the way your money is handled. It is important to consider how you feel about your possessions and money and recognize your personal limits. You have a right to respect whatever is your personal limit. For example, Lori may feel fine with allowing friends to borrow clothes or books but is never comfortable loaning money. In her codependency, she may have loaned money to others even though it made her deeply uneasy, but now, as she is recovering, she consistently tells others no when they request to borrow money.

PHYSICAL

Physical limits are about your body, including safety, affection, and comments and expectations about your body. Physical violence is a clear violation of physical boundaries. Sometimes we may want to set limits on cultural expectations regarding the body, too. There are also issues of violation of physical space by others. It is important to hold yourself and others to these limits. Children are often told to respect one another's "bubble," which highlights the need for physical space from others. This need for physical distance can be flexible. For example, Lori may feel at ease being affectionate with someone she has been dating for some time but is not comfortable having a man she just met sit close to her and touch her thigh. One strategy for setting limits on our physical space is by using cues, like closing the door at home or at the office, or wearing headphones while working.

MENTAL OR EMOTIONAL

When our mental and emotional boundaries are intact, we acknowledge we have the right to make our own choices, the right to our own reality, and the right to our own emotions, no matter how others react. We have the right to believe what is honest for us, but we also have the right to change our belief systems. For example, we may be affiliated with one political party throughout our lives, but over time, we may choose to change our mind. We validate our emotions and the right to our reality. With healthy mental boundaries, we protect our own beliefs while not pushing them onto others. For example, Lori may be very passionate about her religious views, but because she respects that a close friend doesn't feel the same way, she avoids discussing religion with him.

We also know we have the right to privacy. We can be close and intimate with others while still having our separateness.

It is not about secrets; we just don't have to share our every thought or feeling to have true intimacy.

SEXUAL

Boundaries relating to one's sexual self may be very dependent on the relationship, time, and setting. For example, you may have a close sexual partner you trust, but you may not want to have sex at your parents' house while on holiday. With healthy sexual boundaries, we honor that we never owe anyone our sexuality. Furthermore, we protect our sexual health through honest conversations and safer sex practices. Lori wants commitment prior to having a sexual relationship, but she has a tendency to disregard her sexual limits. Unfortunately, when we disregard our personal limits—may they be emotional, physical, or sexual—we often feel hurt, angry, and victimized when the truth is that we did not protect *ourselves*, which was our responsibility.

Asserting Boundaries

One of the hardest—but most rewarding—parts of codependency recovery is the practice of asserting our boundaries. This act requires self-awareness, the commitment to self-respect and acknowledgment of our inherent worthiness, and relearning effective ways of communicating. Many codependents struggle with clear, assertive communication and rely too heavily on passive or passive-aggressive ways of sharing needs, feelings, and limits.

When we assert our boundaries, we tap into our sense of empowerment and control in the world. We cannot control others, but we absolutely have power over honoring our own limits. After beginning to set boundaries, many people have told me they had no idea it would be so liberating. Ultimately, it takes far less physical and emotional energy to have healthy boundaries than to cope without them. We avoid the buildup of stress and resentment and no longer get stuck in our obsessive thoughts about the worst-case scenario, because we assert ourselves more often in the moment. We no longer give ourselves the time to catastrophize or script others' responses in our attachment. When we honor our limits, we are living with integrity as well, which reinforces self-respect.

BE CLEAR

When we are learning how to assert ourselves, we may want to give lengthy explanations or apologies for our boundaries. However, they are most effective when they are succinct, so we do not weaken our position or confuse the other person. The more you can speak up in the moment, the clearer things will be. For example, if Lori's date makes a "joke" that she is dumb, she can clearly state, "Please don't joke about my intelligence; it hurts my feelings."

REACT APPROPRIATELY

Others may sometimes challenge our limits by not respecting them or questioning their validity. Remember, you have the right to your personal limits even if someone says they don't feel the same way. When this happens, remember to be clear and consistent. If Lori's date tells her to stop being so sensitive, as it was just a joke, she can take a deep breath and remind herself that she has the right to not allow others to speak disrespectfully to her. She can then clearly state again, "I understand that you may not have meant to hurt me, but name-calling is hurtful no matter the context. I'm asking you to please respect this." A mindfulness practice can help us stay grounded even if others violate our boundaries. No matter someone's interpretation of our boundary, we are responsible to protect our own limits.

A Picture of Healthy Boundaries

Codependent relationships can be repaired, and it is essential to focus on your own personal boundaries while practicing detachment. When we set and focus on our boundaries, it can be scary— sometimes those relationships may end if the other person doesn't respect them. However, it's likely that we will make a positive impact on our loved ones. I'll illustrate this below.

My mother had me as a teenager and often treated me as a peer. For example, she would reveal far too much about the adult situations in my family. Given this, I also did not respect her limits, and I felt out of control and powerless. When I finally moved out after I graduated from college, I had a lot of pain, resentment, and con- fusion toward her. I did not know how to make sense of this while maintaining a relationship, so I set an extreme boundary in which I did not communicate with her for a year. I had no idea what my mother would do during this time, but I prioritized my healing.

When we reconciled, I discovered my mother took this sepa- ration as a time to focus on her own healing and to seek personal therapy. Since then, my mother has been deeply committed to her ongoing recovery work, like I have been. When I took time to heal, I had no idea what reconciliation would look like with her.

In respecting each other's boundaries, I now have the close but respectful relationship with my mother that I once feared was impossible.

While becoming interdependent with my mother has been an amazing gift for me, I must note that not all relationships heal when we set healthy boundaries. Other people have the right to change—or not change—and when you set boundaries, you are inviting them to change with you to make the relationship healthier, but they are not obligated to do so. All people have the right to decide their values and make their own decisions. Unfortunately, I lost a few relationships when I decided to commit to maintaining healthy boundaries, because they wanted me to love them in a way that wasn't compatible with loving myself.

BE STEADFAST

Initially, setting and maintaining boundaries requires a lot of commitment and effort, but I promise, the payoff in terms of energy, self-respect, and healthier relationships is worth it. You have shown that you are capable and strong in your codependency. It takes incredible dedication to care for others the way a codependent does, and that energy can be directed to the self. When embarking on this change, though, remember to take it one step at a time, and continue to practice self-care to nurture yourself throughout this hard work.

Let Go of Perfectionism

When we are setting boundaries, self-compassion is important. There's no perfect way to set boundaries. When we are learning what our limits are, we still may not always speak up in the moment, or we may let things go that really matter to us. It is important to remember a phrase often said in 12-step meetings: "Progress, not perfection."

I used to strive for perfection in my healing, to never have "off" moments or reactive moments, but I have come to realize that healthy people recognize their limits rather than expect total perfection and enlightenment. Recognizing our limits can be simple. It can be canceling plans with your sister, who tends to ask you to save her from crises, if you are feeling moody one day and don't trust you are up to the task of maintaining your boundaries. Honoring our limits may also mean acknowledging that no matter how many boundaries we set, if the other person is not respectful, some relationships will never allow us to be our best, most loving, authentic self.

EXERCISE: Establishing and Asserting Boundaries

Identify a situation in your life that would benefit from boundaries. Think about what you most fundamentally need from the situation, and then write down one to three short and clear sentences summarizing this. Identify whom you need to speak to about it. Practice this with a person you trust. Repeat this exercise, with different people and in different situations, as many times as needed, until asserting boundaries feels more natural.

Example:

Lori has come to realize that recycling her ex-boyfriends has led to more pain than joy. She realizes she needs to be responsible and stop giving them chances to hurt her. One afternoon, Paul, whom Lori has dated on and off for five years, gives her a call. Usually, she would jump at the opportunity to connect with him, even if it was short-lived; however, she remembers the limit she personally committed to. This is how their conversation goes:

PAUL: I really miss you. We have so much fun together, you know?

LORI: I miss you, too, and we have had a lot of fun together in the past, but it also always ends up with you being unwilling to commit.

PAUL: You know how I feel about you, and the past is the past! This could really be our chance! You just need to spend some time with me to know that I'm serious this time.

LORI: I really care about you and have hoped for years this would happen. You've even told me the same thing before, only to turn around and expect it to remain casual. I won't do that again. It's not healthy for me. I think it's best if we don't talk.

PAUL: Come on, Lori, you can't mean that!

LORI: Yes, I do, Paul. I wish you well, but I have to go. Goodbye.

This was painful for Lori. She didn't want to end things with Paul, but deep down, she's known for a long time that this pattern is unhealthy for her. Lori also feels relief because finally, through her own commitment to self-protection, she broke out of the painful cycle she was in with him.

Not all boundary-setting conversations will be so final. They can be simple, such as "Can you take me to the airport Thursday?" "No, I am working at that time." Or "I know that I have often helped out late at night for your work responsibilities, but I'm no longer able to do that."

Defusing Boundary Testers

It can be scary to set limits, as we do not know how others will respond. Some people will respect our limits, while others will test us. When we set limits that were not previously there, we disrupt homeostasis, so we can expect resistance. Setting boundaries with a healthy person may result in a little pushback, but eventually, a new normal is established. In an unhealthy relationship, this process can be a bit more challenging. Learning how to set boundaries is like building a muscle; when tested, it may require more strength and endurance. Therefore, I encourage you to find the people you can safely set boundaries with initially and practice with them.

STAY FIRM

Along with setting limits, we must establish natural consequences for those who violate them. For example, if you have a friend who consistently runs late because they know you'll wait, you could ask them to please respect your time. Then, if they are more than 15 minutes late in the future, you may leave, to show them that your limits matter to you.

It is also important to note that perhaps you will feel tempted to violate your own limits at times. When we are still developing self-respect, we may feel our own boundaries are inconvenient or not worth setting. Or we may even feel a sense of thrilling rebellion by breaking our rules (such as returning to an unhealthy relationship). Of course, in the end, violating our personal limits only causes future pain, so as often as we can, we must be clear, consistent, and firm with ourselves.

DON'T ALLOW ABUSE

Abuse can take multiple forms in a relationship, including cruelty, violence, and threats. It can be physical, emotional, verbal, or sexual. Unfortunately, some forms of abuse can appear normal, such as threatening to leave, name-calling, or coercing a partner to have sex. For example, a couple may get into intense arguments where they make threats or insult one another. But abuse is unacceptable. If they both agree that this is hurtful and inappropriate, they can make a commitment to intervene when they observe this behavior. They may even choose to attend couples counseling to show their commitment to eliminating abuse. A healthy relationship is free of abuse.

Some forms of abuse are incredibly dangerous physically or emotionally. If there is physical violence, or if sexual abuse is present in a relationship, it is important to create a plan that either removes you (and your children) from it or removes the perpetrator from the home. This can be incredibly scary and even financially difficult, but there are resources to help. If you find yourself in this situation, my heart is with you and I encourage you to reach out to the National Domestic Violence Hotline at 1-800-799-7233 for guidance and support.

One of the hallmarks of codependency is minimizing or denying our personal truth, and because of this, it is sometimes common to live with abuse for a long time before we allow ourselves to see the reality of our relationships. It takes incredible courage to see our relationships with those we love as abusive or unhealthy, because seeing this pushes us to make change, which is scary. I want to reinforce that while abusive relationships can convince you otherwise, there absolutely are healthy people in this world that will value you and your limits. You may already have at least one person like this in your life. It is important to affirm, "I'm worthy of healthy relationships and respect," when eliminating abusive behavior in your life.

Finally, it is important to remember that the way someone responds to your boundaries gives you some important information. If a person continues to violate your boundaries, it is a form of abuse. A person's unwillingness to respect your boundaries shows you their character and is not a reflection of your personal worth.

LET GO OF SELFISHNESS AND GUILT

Selfishness means you place yourself and your needs above someone else. Setting boundaries is not selfish. Healthy boundary setting comes from a place of equality. It is the recognition that you both have equal worth and value. Of course, even understanding the importance of boundaries, you may continue to feel guilt. Setting boundaries is about protecting yourself instead of being too accommodating to others.

"You weren't stupid for getting into and stuck in bad relationships and situations; you just didn't love yourself enough or see your worth. Forgive your younger self for thinking so little of you. From now on, move forward in life, with love for yourself and aware of your worth. This will give you the ability to walk away from those who, for whatever reason, just don't see it."
—*Doe Zantamata*

TAKE IT FURTHER

In this chapter, we have explained what boundaries are, along with the benefits of implementing them, even though this work may seem daunting at times. You have been asked to contemplate your personal limits and identify ways to begin to communicate your boundaries.

To expand on the work of this step, consider the following:

1. It takes immense courage to set healthy boundaries. After all, if you trusted that you were worth more, you would have been able to assert boundaries in the past. What is a limit you have been denying that you have needed to set for a long time but haven't because it's too painful to manage? Journal about this limit while reflecting on this quote popularized by the website Lessons Learned in Life: "One of the most courageous decisions you'll ever make is to finally let go of what is hurting your heart and soul." In addition to this, journal about the nonnegotiable limits you are discovering, such as "They must never call me names" or "My time needs to be respected."

2. Please identify the two safest people to start to make changes with in your life. Note these people in your journal, and list one to three limits or needs you would consider expressing to them. Use the exercise Establishing and Asserting Boundaries (page 91) to identify ways to communicate these boundaries.

3. Finally, guilt is common during this process. To help alleviate it, reflect on this affirmation: "I can love someone and still set limits." Has anyone ever expressed a boundary with you and you recognized it was coming from a place of mutual respect? The same can be true for you.

Step 4
Maintain Open Communication

Carla, 28, recently moved away from her close-knit family due to her husband's promotion. The opportunity was too good for him to pass up. The move also takes them closer to his family (they lived next door to Carla's mother before). Even though Carla and her mother communicate at least three times a day, her mother frequently tells Carla she misses her and that she should come back. Carla often stays quiet, knowing that her mother just needs to express her disappointment. Beyond that, her family very strongly adheres to the adage, "Respect your elders."

However, when they get off the phone, Carla notices feelings of irritation and anxiety thinking about speaking to her mother again. Carla wants to be a supportive wife, but her mother's guilt-tripping is making her wonder how to keep everyone happy. When she turns to her husband, Andres, for support, he looks at her with irritation and tells her to get over it because they lived next to her family for five years and things need to be fair. Her husband has never really cared to talk to her about her feelings as he says she can be too emotional. Carla has also been concerned lately about a friendship he is developing with his colleague, Diane. Before the move, Andres made it a point to come home after work to relax with Carla, but lately, he's been finding reasons to stay late at the office or claiming he must attend happy hour to bond with his coworkers. Carla knows that Diane is always at these events or in the office, as Andres often mentions things she did or said. Carla has asked him about their relationship, but he tells her to stop being so paranoid and that he thinks she has too much free time on her hands—she needs to get a hobby now that she's away from family.

Carla hasn't told her mother, best friend, or cousin—the three people she usually tells everything to—about any of these concerns because she is afraid of their feedback and negative judgments of her husband. Carla is hoping the issues resolve on their own. Since Carla has been holding in more of her worries, she has been noticing she is having a hard time focusing and sleeping.

Common Communication Issues

Communication can be understood as an exchange of information. It's what we say and what we hear as well as how we say it and what we observe. There are numerous ways communication can go awry, and one or all parties involved can walk away from an interaction feeling misunderstood. Below are some common issues in communication.

INDIRECT COMMUNICATION

Often, codependents feel afraid that their emotions or needs will be burdensome to others, and so they develop an indirect way of communicating. With indirect communication, a person will avoid discussing their thoughts, feelings, and desires because they may feel they are inconvenient and don't want their individual perspective to cause any issues. A passive way of communicating can become automatic when we learn to minimize or deny our concerns even to ourselves. Sometimes, in codependency, we may stifle our feelings to avoid making our concerns real. We may even tell ourselves we are wrong to have these concerns in the first place and will therefore never address them.

PASSIVE AND PASSIVE-AGGRESSIVE COMMUNICATION

A person may believe that if they directly ask for something and are told no, they will not be able to tolerate that disappointment. In codependency, it can often feel like you are "owed" a yes if you faced your fears and did the hard work of asking directly for a need to be met. In reality, every person has the right to honestly meet or decline a request. This inability to cope with disappointment if we do the hard work of speaking up can lead to passive-aggressive communication. This is a type of indirect communication in which we may drop hints but still will not say what we want outright. Often, people who communicate in this way are expecting the other person to guess what they need. However, most of us are not good at understanding indirect communication, as by its very nature it is unclear. Therefore, when the other person guesses incorrectly, a passive-aggressive communicator will continue to act on their resentment. They may even continue to give cues that they are upset, such as eye rolling or sighing, but, when asked what's wrong, will state that everything is fine.

COMMUNICATION AS A MEANS TO CONTROL

Using communication as a means to control may arise from the stress of stifling or minimizing feelings over time, until you feel that you can't hold these intense feelings in any longer. Like a bucket, there's only so much we can contain until we overflow—in extreme cases, this overflow may lead to explosive and aggressive behavior. And aggressive communication, even without ill intent, is often abusive.

Since the 1970s, researcher John Gottman has been studying what leads to happy marriages and what behaviors lead to divorce. Through his research, Gottman defined four separate behaviors that, above all others, predict divorce. Nicknamed "the Four Horsemen of the Apocalypse," these behaviors are criticism, contempt, defensiveness, and stonewalling. Here I will focus on criticism as a form of controlling communication.

Criticism is different from negative feedback in that in many cases, negative feedback is necessary in healthy, interdependent relationships. After all, we may at times feel hurt by someone or disappointed, and as we recover, it is important to address this with the other person in a balanced and respectful way. Criticism, on the other hand, is often marked by comments that another person "always" or "never" does something and sends the message that the offender is universally wrong. For example, most of us will feel hurt, angry, or defensive if a friend tells us, "You never consider me and always cancel at the last minute." Harsh criticism doesn't give the recipient many options to help resolve the conflict in a manner that's beneficial for both parties. In the above scenario, if your response is "But I don't always cancel at the last minute," the friend will feel invalidated, and this further extends the miscommunication.

Another common form of controlling communication is threats. By using threats, a person is trying to force the other person into doing something. This desire may be rooted in a legitimate need, but threatening language is coercive and inappropriate.

GASLIGHTING

The history of this term dates back to a play, *Gas Light*, in which a husband intentionally tries to convince his wife that she is going insane. In modern times, gaslighting is understood as an attempt to control others by confusing them about reality. A gaslighter may lie or deny they ever did or said something, even if you have proof to the contrary. Within the bounds of codependency, reality is often already confusing or unclear, which may cause a codependent to tolerate this kind of behavior for longer than others. This further reinforces feelings of confusion and shame. Shame is a common response to gaslighting because this behavior includes an element of scapegoating the recipient. The message is that if you weren't so flawed, then you wouldn't question the other person. This is what happens when Andres tells Carla she is being paranoid. It is unclear what Andres's behavior changes mean, but if he were able to communicate in a healthy, interdependent manner, he would be able to validate Carla's concerns. He could say something like, "I have been spending a lot of time with Diane after work, so I can see why you are feeling curious or jealous."

When interacting with others who use manipulative tactics, it's easy to believe you are the problem. If only you weren't so sensitive, then the other person would behave appropriately. In actuality, both of you have a right to your boundaries and nonnegotiable needs, and you and the other person are either willing or unwilling to meet them.

COMMUNICATION AS PROTECTION

Ideally, we use boundaries to protect ourselves and communication to share ourselves with others. In codependency, when we lack healthy boundaries, we may use ineffective communication strategies in an attempt to self-protect, and being secretive is one of these unhealthy strategies. For example, if you do not want to lose a relationship or face a negative consequence because of someone else's boundaries or concerns, you may lie or be secretive. If Carla doesn't want to hear her best friend's feedback about her husband's dismissive behavior, she may lie that everything is great in their marriage. We can also see that Andres may be doing the same thing by not directly addressing Carla's questions.

It should be noted that defensive communication arises from feeling overly vulnerable. Without healthy boundaries, even neutral feedback or attempts to problem solve can feel like personal attacks. This pain leads people to act out in disrespectful ways. Defensiveness is used to protect one's self from a perceived attack, rather than caring about resolution of conflict to improve the relationship. Furthermore, defensiveness often invalidates the recipient. We can see this in Carla and Andres's interactions regarding his colleague. His primary goal is self-protection rather than exploring Carla's perspective, his own, and ways to work toward resolution.

When defensive, it is also common to make jokes at someone's expense, mock them, or be sarcastic. Defensiveness often crosses the line into contempt, which sends the message that one person in the relationship is better than the other. People often act defensively to protect against the vulnerability of looking at their own role in conflict. If Andres mocks Carla for being too emotional, then he doesn't have to consider how his own reactions may evoke intense emotions in her.

Restorative Communication

Effective communication occurs when we clearly state what we want, actively listen for feedback, and are willing to clarify and negotiate our perspectives and needs. When we communicate in an interdependent manner, there are no ulterior motives. Of course, we still have desires or needs of others, but when interdependent, we state them while accepting that the other person may or may not be willing or able to give us what we want. Every person has the right to say no—including you.

Identifying and Managing Triggers

To maintain open communication, it's necessary to develop awareness of your tendencies to be passive, passive-aggressive, or aggressive but to also notice that sometimes certain people or circumstances may make it more difficult to communicate effectively. Learning to identify your personal triggers is an important step in establishing healthier communication strategies. Reflect on your day. Were there situations, times of day, or certain people that elicited more passive, passive-aggressive, or aggressive communication from you? Did you react in a hostile way to someone who regularly makes your heart race or gives you tension in your neck or shoulders?

In your journal, write down your personal triggers. Look them over after you are done. If you notice that certain situations trigger negative behavior, then in similar situations in the future, it may be helpful to take a break. Give yourself the space to pause, use your coping skills, and then revisit the conversation when you can speak clearly again. The goal in identifying your triggers is to learn how to practice self-care as needed to manage them more effectively, rather than just avoiding the interactions. For example, you may need to practice coping skills before or after talking to your ex-spouse or boss. This is completely normal. Certain conversations are still important for you to have, but you can learn to manage your triggers to communicate more effectively.

It is important to note that in general, physical issues, such as being sleep-deprived, hungry, or in physical pain, can make it much more challenging to have healthy conversations. We cannot always avoid these physical triggers, but once we are aware of them, we can be mindful of caring for them. You could add improving sleep to your self-care plan, or keep snacks in your desk at work. It may sound too simple, but I have learned that I can maintain my improved way of communicating with my mother when I don't call her around my lunchtime. Hunger makes me irritable, and given our history of communicating ineffectively, it can be easier for me to snap at her than at someone else. I do not want to behave this way, so I make sure I've eaten prior to returning her call.

Assertive communication is respectful and requires us to be honest about who we are and what we need. When we communicate assertively, we live with integrity. We say what we mean, and we mean what we say. We know that we have both the responsibility and the right to advocate for ourselves.

NONVIOLENT COMMUNICATION

Nonviolent communication, or NVC, provides an effective alternative to resorting to passive-aggression or aggression when stuck in disagreement. Marshall Rosenberg developed the model of NVC in the 1960s. This model includes four components— observation, feeling, needs, and request—as well as two parts, empathy and honesty. The basic outline is to say something like, "When I see [state what you are observing without judgment or interpretations], I feel [state emotion] because my need for [state personal need] is unmet. Would you be willing to [restate personal need]?" Carla could use this with Andres, for example, regarding their conversations about her mother. She could say to him, "When I see you become irritable when I bring up my mother, I feel hurt because my need to be listened to by you isn't being met. Would you be willing to just listen to me sometimes when I vent about my mother?" When we use NVC, we cannot ensure that the other person will respond in a way we prefer, but using this approach will likely allow them to be less defensive with us than when we attack or criticize them.

In a healthy relationship, the perspective shifts from one where each person is their own team to one in which both parties within the relationship are on the same team. They may have different needs or goals at times, but as a team, they prioritize the relationship with a willingness to be assertive and negotiate to find a resolution that meets both persons' needs. For example, Carla may want to communicate with her mother daily but not three times a day, as her mother prefers. Carla could then tell her mother that she loves connecting but that she needs time to focus on work and then ask to speak just once daily. Her mother may then ask if this is flexible on weekends, when she's not working, and Carla may be open to compromising here.

AVOID ASSUMPTIONS

We can only guess what another person is thinking, and often, due to our insecurities and negative belief systems, we guess incorrectly. The reality is that we can't know what another person is thinking or feeling if we do not ask. For example, Carla may walk into her supervisor's office with a simple question when her supervisor lets out a sigh. Carla may think this indicates that her supervisor considers her a bother and that she should not ask her question but instead try to find the answer elsewhere. In reality, her supervisor may have been sighing due to a spreadsheet that she had grown tired of looking at just as Carla walked into her office. If Carla were to use assertive communication skills, she could simply ask her supervisor if this is an okay time for them to have a quick conversation or if they should find another time.

WATCH YOUR TONE AND BODY LANGUAGE

Communication is also expressed through nonverbal cues—eye contact, tone of voice, and posture. It's necessary to read nonverbal aspects of communication to understand fully what another person is trying to convey. After all, most of us can relate to being uncertain of how to interpret a text or an e-mail precisely because there were no nonverbal cues about the sender's intention. It is important to be mindful of your posture, tone, and eye contact, and make sure they are congruent with what you are saying. The way we deliver a message impacts the way it is received, regardless of our intention. I often hear couples and families argue over someone's yelling. The person who has been described as yelling will often argue that they were not yelling. How you are perceived matters for effective communication. Even if you don't believe you are shouting, if someone feels you have taken an escalated tone with them, they will likely shut down or become aggressive. Here's a simple example of the importance of having our nonverbal and verbal communication match: If your spouse tells you they appreciated the dinner you cooked while staring at the TV, it's likely it won't feel as sincere as if they had turned directly to you while giving you eye contact and saying the same thing.

DON'T LECTURE

In the past, whenever I felt disappointed with other people, I thought it was appropriate to continually tell them how they were not meeting my needs. I did not understand how else to have my needs met without constantly repeating myself. Finally, a good friend told me the secret: Share what hurt us or what we need clearly and respectfully while allowing the other person a chance to meet our needs or not to. They may disappoint us again, but we do not have the right to lecture them. Instead, we have the responsibility to clarify our personal limits and the responsibility to implement consequences for violating them. Instead of delivering harsh criticism, as discussed earlier in this step (Common Communication Issues, page 97), we want to clearly state a complaint and then be open to negotiation.

EXERCISE: Communication Script

Effective and assertive communication can be accomplished with a few sentences. Read the following examples of ineffective and more effective communication between Carla and her mother. Then, in your journal, write down a personal situation that would benefit from improved communication. You may even have examples of times a conversation hasn't gone well that you can transcribe to help troubleshoot where your communication style goes awry. Prior to having another stressful conversation, outline what you feel and most basically need or want from the other person. Write this out in one or two clear sentences. Remember, though, that when you share these clear statements, your goal is to be better understood. You cannot control the other person—they may or may not meet your request, but that will be important information.

INEFFECTIVE:

MOTHER: You're so far away now.

CARLA: I know, Mom. It's really awful.

MOTHER: It is awful. I mean, I'm getting older now. Just yesterday, I was walking up the stairs and I felt like my bad hip might give out. You know, your brother is busy with his wife. I don't know who will help me if I fall now.

CARLA: Mom, please don't say that.

MORE EFFECTIVE:

MOTHER: I just can't believe you are so far away.

CARLA: I understand you miss me, and I miss you, too.

MOTHER: I just feel like life is too short to be away from each other.

CARLA: Mom, I feel sad and concerned being so far away from you, but it is important to me to support Andres right now. I do want to schedule a visit soon. I have a three-day weekend coming up—do you think that may work for you?

MOTHER: That's still not enough time.

CARLA: Yes, I know, three days is not very long, but we miss each other, and I don't have paid time off yet. I'm hoping we can make this work.

Let's take a moment to compare these two conversations. We can see Carla's mother attempt to make Carla feel guilty. In the first example, Carla's open boundaries leave her vulnerable to this guilt. In the second example, we see Carla being honest and direct with her mother without capitulating to her demands. Carla may not be able to control how her mother feels and behaves, but she can control how she herself communicates.

BE PATIENT

We have a lifetime of practicing indirect or aggressive forms of communication. It takes time to learn how to become more effective in our communication, because not only are we not in the practice of using assertive communication, but effective communication also requires a combination of skills, including self-awareness, healthy boundaries, and ongoing self-care. Given that establishing healthy communication is complex, I encourage you to practice patience and self-compassion above all else. Just like practicing any new skill, mistakes are part of the learning process.

Communication Troubleshooting

Communication can go awry at times even when we practice skills to communicate more kindly and assertively, such as with NVC, and are mindful of our triggers. After all, human beings are imperfect, so even in recovery, we cannot always have perfect interactions. However, we can develop strategies to help steer our interactions back on course when misunderstanding arises, so that we can maintain our self-respect as well as protect our relationship. Below are some strategies to further improve your efficacy when interacting with others.

LEARNING TO WALK AWAY

It is a fact that when we are intensely emotional, we can no longer think clearly. We have both a sympathetic and a parasympathetic nervous system. The former allows us to notice perceived danger, while the latter allows us to calm down and relax. The sympathetic nervous system allows us to act quickly in fight-or-flight mode when we perceive a threat in order to stay safe. During these times, the kindest and most effective thing we can do is take a break from an emotional conversation. Let the other person know that you need a moment to calm down, and ask if you can revisit the conversation in 20 minutes, or as much time as you need, but you *must* return to continue the conversation. During your break, use healthy coping skills, such as aromatherapy, guided meditation, coloring, yoga, or journaling. These gentle activities send the message to your body that it is now safe, so your parasympathetic nervous system can relax you. After your break, you will notice that you are better able to communicate your perspective assertively and resolve concerns in an interdependent manner.

BREAKING OUT OF ROLES TO COMMUNICATE AUTHENTICALLY

Complicating the development of assertive communication are roles—those assigned to us by our families as well as gender roles. There are emotions that are allowed and disapproved of in men and women. Men may be seen as weak if they discuss feelings of pain, rejection, or embarrassment, whereas women are perceived as hysterical, crazy, or bitchy for discussing anger. As we recover, we can acknowledge that emotions do not show up more in either gender and that we have a right to all our emotions. Furthermore, while there may be rules or roles in our family that prohibit us from talking honestly and directly, we want to work to break out of these false roles. We practice self-compassion and validating the truth of our emotions because they are fundamental components to who we are authentically.

LEARN TO TALK ABOUT COMMUNICATION

Learning to communicate about communication can be transformative. When we do, we can highlight which ways of communicating work for us in our relationship and which don't. We can comment on how we interpret the other person, at times, from a mindful and nonjudgmental perspective. We want to work on expressing what we are noticing without being contemptuous. For example, if the person you are speaking to makes a few sarcastic comments, you may want to say, "I've noticed that you keep making sarcastic jokes at my expense tonight, which is hurtful, but it also makes me wonder if something is going on between us that we should talk about." When we comment on the communication mindfully—noticing what is happening without being judgmental—we can transform interactions in the moment. The more we comment in the moment, the less often we will need follow-up conversations to restore the relationship, because the repair happened in real time. This ability is so empowering!

MANAGE DEFENSIVE REACTIONS

It is very common to feel embarrassed or ashamed when we feel misunderstood, feel invalidated, or have negatively impacted someone else. Healthy self-esteem means accepting our imperfections, understanding that imperfection is human and completely okay. While it is never our intention to be hurtful or offensive, the reality is that we can come across as such even when practicing communication skills. At these times, we want to practice self-compassion and work on being curious about the other person's perspective. To maintain self-respect, we want to acknowledge our role in conflict but not apologizing in a blanket way. Instead, we remember we are on the same team, and the more we resolve things interdependently, the stronger the team. We acknowledge the other person's perspective, share ours kindly, and remember the power of authentic apologies. We live in a culture that doesn't often reflect honest apologies. We often see people defend and deny rather than acknowledge their role in difficult situations. It takes incredible maturity, self-compassion, and a healthy sense of self to apologize when we have been hurtful or offensive. Ironically, too, the more we take appropriate accountability, the healthier our sense of self, as we notice that being imperfect is not the end of the world. It's okay, and usually, other people want to continue to repair things with us, which helps us see our true worth.

EXERCISE: Challenging Anxious Thoughts

Many of us have been indirect in our speech or overly aggressive due to the fear that we can't get our needs met or we won't be respected. Think about why you have communicated passively or passive-aggressively in the past. What were you afraid of if you spoke the truth? For example, you may have been afraid to ask the person you were dating if they wanted to be exclusive because they might say no. This exercise can be completed in your journal any time you are nervous about having a conversation.

Think about a current situation you are afraid or nervous to address:

What's the worst-case scenario?
If the worst-case scenario happens, how will I cope?
What is a more likely outcome?
How will I cope?
What is the benefit of speaking up no matter the outcome?

TAKE IT FURTHER

In this step, we discussed common barriers to healthy, assertive communication. You were asked to reflect on your own communication styles that may interfere with effective interaction. Improving our communication styles and patterns takes practice and patience but is possible with commitment and mindfulness. Remember, although it can be scary to advocate for ourselves, it is our responsibility and right in our recovery.

Moving forward, to continue to improve your communication, please consider the following:

1. Continue building awareness of your codependent communication behaviors and your triggers so you can interrupt them more often. To do this, pay attention to how you communicate with the people in your life. Then, work on managing your responses by slowing down (remind yourself to breathe during interactions) and taking breaks from conversations if you do not feel capable of responding effectively in the moment. It is not only healthy but also physiologically imperative to take breaks from conversations if needed.

2. Continue to practice self-awareness, daily self-care, and commitment to healthy boundaries—effective communication requires all of these. We have to know what we need, set healthy boundaries, and cope effectively with the stress of beginning to assert ourselves along with whatever emotions may arise from an interaction. Be gentle with yourself and have realistic expectations, as healing communication is complex. To hold on to those realistic expectations, reflect on your triggers and remember that these situations and/or relationships may well be difficult—but not impossible—to deal with. Don't use triggering situations as measures of success.

3. Deepak Chopra said, "Every time you are tempted to react in the same old way, ask if you want to be a prisoner of the past or a pioneer of the future." It can't be said enough—it will take time to become an assertive communicator, but every time you are assertive now is a success. When you notice you respond assertively in a situation that would have been difficult for you in the past, please take a moment to celebrate yourself for being a pioneer in your recovered future!

Step 5
Nurture Intimacy

Sarah, 53, and Patrick, 55, have been together for 25 years. Early in their marriage, they had fun and were committed to their shared goals related to family. While Patrick worked, Sarah stayed home and raised their two boys. Over time, they began living more separate lives. Patrick became more involved in his company, while Sarah focused on the childcare and volunteering at school events. Eventually, Sarah began to feel like they were strangers. Throughout the years, Sarah tried to discuss this feeling with Patrick. He sometimes noticed the pain and shame of no longer having fun with his wife. He saw his parents living quiet lives of resignation, and so although he wanted something different, he didn't know how to create it. Furthermore, he had been raised to view emotions as weakness, so he would dismiss these concerns. Inadvertently, this led to Sarah feeling invalidated, so she eventually resigned herself to feeling disconnected. Over the years, she spent more time confiding in her best friend, Kate.

Sarah deeply values her religious commitments, and for her, divorce is not an option, but she is dissatisfied. Now she sees some of her friends entering early retirement and having fun traveling with their spouses. Sarah feels lost as her youngest son, Peter, is graduating from high school this year. Both Sarah and Patrick feel alone in their marriage, but at this point, neither knows how to bridge this gap.

Intimacy in the Codependent Relationship

As we enter recovery, the concept of intimacy can be simultaneously confusing and intimidating. After all, in codependency, we often both crave intimacy and fear it. Negative beliefs about our personal worth can lead us to believe that ultimately, we will be abandoned or rejected, and if this happens, we won't be able to tolerate it. Culturally, intimacy is understood to occur primarily in romantic or sexual relationships. But this is inaccurate—the most basic definition of intimacy is about closeness and friendship. When we notice this, our understanding and experience of intimacy becomes expansive. There is the opportunity to have numerous interdependently intimate relationships in our lives. This can also help us feel more hopeful that we can deepen our ability to connect with others. After all, you may already have someone in your life you feel especially close to even if they're not a romantic partner. They may be a cousin, your parent, or a best friend.

EMOTIONAL GUARDING

Before we learn our value and how to be interdependently intimate, it is common to hide our true self from others. We hide or guard who we are to deal with the discomfort of vulnerability. We can do this in a couple of ways. First, we can guard against vulnerability in our communication styles, as seen in the previous step. Shutting someone out, defensiveness, and contempt act like armor and weapons for the person utilizing these tactics.

These communication styles allow us to feel less exposed as we are placing ourselves above someone else, but they are also very damaging to the relationship. You cannot find and establish intimate relationships with people if you don't risk revealing who you authentically are. You must commit to removing your masks so your people can recognize you.

LACK OF DEMONSTRATED AFFECTION

Touch is essential to our well-being. However, this is a need that we cannot fully meet independently, so we must receive affection from our loved ones. This reality highlights the truth that we are designed to be interdependent. It can take time to learn how to understand the expression of affection as healthy, safe, and nonsexual touch, especially as our culture can overemphasize affection as existing primarily in sexual or romantic relationships, particularly for men. If you have ever been in the midst of painful loss and grief, you know that sometimes a friend rubbing your back, taking your hand, or hugging you can mean more than words can express. Touch is essential for healthy human development. A study published in 2004 showed that skin-to-skin contact for premature infants had incredible benefits. Children who received loving touch consistently performed better on tests related to cognition as well as executive abilities, from 6 months to 10 years old. Throughout our lives, touch remains important.

HIDING VULNERABILITIES

It can be daunting to reveal who we are. Years ago, a good friend told me that intimacy could be translated to "into me you see." When she said that, I realized why I had been avoiding a healthy, intimate dating relationship. Codependency originates from a place of shame and feeling unworthy the way we authentically are, so vulnerability can be terrifying early in recovery. Therefore, we may believe, "If you see who I really am, then you will automatically reject me." Ultimately, although I do find it scary, I have learned it takes less energy to live in an authentically open and vulnerable manner when I have healthy boundaries intact.

PUSHING AWAY THOSE WHO SHOW YOU AFFECTION

In my most painfully codependent relationship, I remember once crying to my partner that he only gave me crumbs. He corrected me—he told me he didn't even give me crumbs—and I accepted that. For a long time, I internalized that I wasn't worth even crumbs, and I attracted more unhealthy relationships. Over time, I realized that just because I *felt* I wasn't worthwhile didn't mean this was absolute truth and fact. When we have negative self-views, it is common to push away those who treat us with respect and kindness. I would often think that something must be wrong with a man if he expressed interest in me. When I didn't like myself, I found it much easier to spend time with men who treated me unkindly because we had a common enemy: me.

It seems ironic to me that it takes so much courage to learn to let love in, but it is true nonetheless. I think this is explained by a discovery made by Brené Brown. She found that it's our most beautiful moments—such as getting engaged or having a child—that can activate the most pain of vulnerability. In these moments, we see what we can lose. The goal, she shares, is to lean into our moments of joy in the face of vulnerability rather than shut down, as many of us do. Learning to let love in takes a lot of courage, but we can begin this work by noticing the areas in your life where you already do this, such as with your best friends or your mother.

EXERCISE: You Are Enough

Intimacy can be complicated by negative self-views. Not only do they increase our willingness to tolerate unkind or disrespectful behavior, but they also can create a desire for someone else's approval. For this exercise, think of the three people you are closest to. On a page in your journal, draw three columns and put one name in each column. Now, contemplate your relationship with them and the positive feedback they have given you. Identify five positive qualities that you believe they would say you possess, and write them in their column. For example, Sarah may make columns for her husband, her best friend, and her oldest son. She will note that all would say she is supportive, her best friend would say she is funny, and her husband would say she is passionate. Now, circle the qualities in each column that you agree reflect your authentic self. From these qualities, develop a statement to remind yourself of the gifts you bring by being you. For example, Sarah may state, "I am a supportive, interesting, and fun person, and I deserve healthy and meaningful relationships." When you come up with your own affirmation, repeat it to yourself when you feel insecure about your deservingness of a good relationship.

Positive Outcomes

Experiencing intimacy is fundamental to good mental and physical health. Ideally, we learn to establish secure attachments to other human beings. We enable secure attachments when we trust completely that the other person will be there for us in times of need and genuinely cares about our well-being. When we have this security, we are more self-confident, take healthy risks in our life, and feel more focused.

The Intimacy–Substance Connection

Substances and intimacy are connected in two common ways: They both numb the pain of disconnection and help us manage the fear of vulnerability. Many people do not know how to manage intimacy in healthy ways, so substances can help them tolerate the vulnerability inherent in building relationships. A very common dating activity is drinking, and I think this is in part because it takes a lot of skill to manage the vulnerability of getting to know someone, and alcohol makes it easier. While sex is not the only form of intimacy, it is an intimate activity, and I have frequently heard young people state that they have never had sober sex. This highlights the fear of vulnerability that is being managed with substances.

On the other side of the coin, disconnection from others is intensely painful. When people lack healthy coping skills, they often find unhealthy ways to dull this pain, whether it is with alcohol, pills, or other drugs. It is important to learn to manage the pain of disconnection and fear of vulnerability in healthy ways to have a more satisfying life. The literal pain of disconnection will be discussed more later on in this step.

Feeling uncomfortable with disconnection is engrained in our physiology, so the work here, rather than numbing the pain, is to find ways to increase connection. Maybe your life is currently quite isolated—that's okay; you can start small in finding ways to build more connection, such as saying hello to the commuter next to you on the subway or chatting with a coworker after a meeting. Other ways to build connection to reduce pain are caring for a pet or volunteering.

HUMANS DESIRE CONNECTION

Attachment theory, developed by psychiatrist John Bowlby, suggests that the desire to belong is just as much a physical need as an emotional one. Consider life in prehistoric times—individuals fared better when living in a community as opposed to being on their own. As humans, we developed a physiological attachment system to stay safe that allows us to feel calm when near those we are connected to and upset when we sense disconnection. Our biology tells us that disconnection threatens our survival, so protest behaviors, such as excessive calling or clinging when we feel disconnected, are not necessarily clues that we are codependent. Codependency is about prioritizing others over our own self, whereas interdependency is the balance of acknowledging our worth and value with our need for connection. We will not harm ourselves for connection, but we know that having healthy relationships is fundamental to a joyful, meaningful life.

LONELINESS HURTS

Loneliness and solitude are different things. Solitude is pleasurable aloneness, an opportunity to enjoy a little "me time." On the other hand, loneliness is the painful disconnection from others. It is important to note that loneliness, as a *sense* of disconnection, can arise even when we have relationships with others, including living with a spouse. For those of us who have experienced feeling lonely in a crowded room, we know just how deeply painful that is. Psychologist Naomi Eisenberger conducted a study that monitored how the brain reacts to social isolation and found the same two areas in the brain that are activated when we are physically hurt are activated when we are socially isolated. In other words, the brain perceives disconnection from others in the same way it perceives physical pain.

Furthermore, loneliness is destructive to our health. In his work on marital stability, Gottman found that lonely husbands married to contemptuous wives were more physically ill than other husbands. And a recent meta-analysis authored by a group of psychology researchers revealed that loneliness has an even greater mortality risk than obesity. We are starting to see that loneliness is literally deadly.

HEALTHY INTIMACY CAN REDUCE STRESS

Healthy intimacy allows us to feel a sense of safety and security in the world. Numerous studies have revealed that from a biological perspective, people who are close become an attached unit—they regulate each other's blood pressure, breathing, and heart rate. You may have experienced this yourself after a long, stressful day when you came home to a loved one and noticed that you could finally relax. Secure attachment helps people feel more self-confident, and this confidence helps increase resiliency in times of crisis. It allows us to know we are capable of coping with the pain and stress we are experiencing in healthy ways. Furthermore, people with a secure attachment are better able to seek support in times of crisis, which, of course, helps reduce stress.

INCREASED EMPATHY

There is a reciprocity with empathy: Close relationships help us develop empathy, and empathy helps us develop close relationships. Empathy is the experience of both understanding and caring about others' emotional reactions and perspectives in the world. The process of becoming more empathetic is sometimes just as simple as truly listening to another human being and acknowledging their experience. We do not always have to have an answer or response to questions, nor do we have to share our perspective. Furthermore, while defensiveness is a common reaction to getting feedback we do not agree with, it tends to keep relationships stuck. Empathy allows us a pathway to deeper understanding and intimacy.

It can be easy to underestimate the power of validation, which is the acknowledgment of someone's truth regardless of what we think or feel about it. This can be done very simply. For example, if Sarah tells Patrick that she feels they are disconnected, he can validate her by repeating back what she says exactly: "What I'm hearing you say, Sarah, is you feel we have become disconnected." Validation allows us to more deeply appreciate the other person's perspective and feelings, which can often lead the receiver of the validation to feel more understood and cared about, which in turn can strengthen the relationship. And at the same time, validating others often enables them to then do the same for us, because they feel a sense of respect and care by our validation.

INCREASED SELF-AWARENESS

The development of self-awareness is ongoing throughout our lives and always beneficial. There is an old saying that knowledge is power. I believe that self-knowledge is deeply empowering. As we have learned, the more deeply you know yourself, the clearer your boundaries and communication. Intimacy allows us to continue to build our relationship with the self, as there are some things we can know about ourselves only when other people give us feedback. For example, Patrick may believe his self-reliance and refusal to acknowledge emotions are a strength, given his childhood, but with Sarah's feedback, he may learn that they are actually preventing him from having a richer, more meaningful life.

Opening to Intimacy

It is my belief that healing many of our relationships is fully possible in recovery. There is the potential for deeper intimacy with numerous people in your life, provided that there is a sense of mutual respect. There can be the fear of being rejected or abandoned when we contemplate intimacy, but it's also common to fear being smothered by another. A popular idea about intimacy maintains that to truly love another, we must experience loss of the self. However, truly healthy intimacy is best represented by a Venn diagram. We are each separate people with our right to private thoughts and feelings, but we also have an overlap where we come together and share who we are so we can each experience joy and connection. In this section, we'll explore some ways to approach healthy intimate connections.

ESTABLISH TRUST

In truth, it takes time to establish trust. Without healthy boundaries, this reality can be very threatening, but the goal is to share who we are over time. We don't hide behind walls, but we also don't tell someone our entire life story immediately, as they haven't earned the privilege of knowing us that deeply yet. We learn, with healthy boundaries, that we do have the ability to discern trustworthy and untrustworthy people over time. This perspective highlights the importance of allowing a relationship to develop naturally and on its own terms. Trust that in time, we will learn if this is a healthy relationship for us or not. The goal of healthy relationships is to develop an unconditional warmth for one another even when we make mistakes.

KEEP YOUR WANTS AND NEEDS IN MIND

In codependency, it is typical to connect to others from an inauthentic place where we stifle our own needs and wants.

Often, this passivity leads to resentment, as we trick ourselves into thinking, "I'll never tell you what I really want because I can't risk that you'll say no. So, I will take what you give me, but I'll resent you for not giving me what I really want." It does require vulnerability to share our needs with someone and risk being disappointed, but it is the pathway to recovery.

PRACTICE ACCEPTANCE

When establishing and maintaining intimacy, it is important to continue to practice detachment. Relationships have a life of their own that cannot follow predetermined personal or cultural outlines of how they must progress. We can have a deeply intimate relationship in which we are mutually important, but this doesn't mean that in day-to-day life we can always prioritize one another perfectly. For example, Sarah may want some of Patrick's time on any given day, but if he is on a work deadline, he may be less available to her. This doesn't mean they can't have a more intimate relationship, but perhaps that week it will be less at the forefront. Intimacy, in its most rewarding state, embodies unconditional love and acceptance of one another. Wanting to change someone to fit into what you desire for them is the opposite of this unconditionally loving state. When we are developing interdependent intimate relationships, we need to remember that we do not have the right to change others. In an intimate relationship, we can influence one another, but we do not have the right to interfere with someone's free will.

Recovery requires a lot of growth and willingness to mature, and it requires a lot of maturity to see and accept our loved ones for who they are rather than our own projections of who we want them to be. However, this willingness to practice acceptance will lead to more rewarding relationships than you can imagine. There is a sense of peace when you are no longer spending your time fixated on how to change someone. You can now focus on just enjoying one another!

EMBRACE AUTHENTICITY

Inauthenticity prevents the intimacy we most crave. We must be a whole person who is internally focused in knowing and valuing our true self to have deep intimacy. Instead of wearing masks and modifying our personalities depending on our audience, we learn how to be flexible in our authentic presentation of self. This means that you are always completely yourself in your interactions, but with healthy boundaries, you realize that not everyone needs to know the same amount of information or will experience the same level of intimacy with you. For example, in Sarah's recovery, she is always herself, but she will show up a little differently with her sons, her husband, and her best friend. Her sons may see her nurturing side, her husband her most passionate side, and her best friend her most playful side. Sarah is always herself in these interactions, but with healthy boundaries, she shares different aspects of herself. The goal is to be who you authentically are no matter what but with healthy boundaries. When we do this, we can end up having more connection—and fun—than we ever imagined possible while we were in codependency.

Finally, I want to note that while intimacy is so much more than sex, some people may have severed their sense of intimacy with sexuality. In reality, some of us may be able to engage in sex without a feeling of intimacy, whereas others may need the feeling of intimacy to enjoy sexual relationships. It is never an accomplishment to sever ties with what is authentic for us regardless of cultural messages. Intimacy requires ongoing check-ins with ourselves about what we value and what our boundaries are.

EXERCISE: Developing Intimacy

No matter how long we have known someone, it is possible to deepen our connection through commitment and open communication. This process requires self-awareness to know what you want in the relationship as well as the willingness and courage to be vulnerable. Prior to having these conversations, we want to identify what we want and then bring that to the other. To illustrate this, let's take a look at a conversation between Sarah and Patrick:

> **SARAH:** Patrick, can we talk about something? *She says this as she sits down next to him and reaches for his hand knowing that while he never has stated it, he often appears more relaxed when they touch.*

> **PATRICK:** What is it? *He takes a deep breath, unsure if she has a complaint.*

> **SARAH:** You know Peter is graduating this year, and I was hoping we could spend this time getting to know each other again.

> **PATRICK:** What do you mean by "getting to know each other"? You're my wife.

> **SARAH:** *She takes a deep breath knowing that it is easy to get defensive.* Of course we know each other, but I miss the way we used to talk when we would get coffee or take walks. You know, like when the boys were little?

> **PATRICK:** *He is able to relax by her staying relaxed.* I haven't thought about those days in a long time, but they were really nice. I'm still not sure what you mean by "getting to know each other." Are you asking for more time together?

Stepping Away from Caretaking

In interdependency, we still absolutely value our relationships, but the goal is to care for others, not carry them. When we try to solve others' problems or do for them what they need to be able to do for themselves, we are carrying them. Furthermore, when we see their lives as problems to fix, we automatically put ourselves in a higher place than them. Instead, in a healthy relationship, two equals come together in mutual respect. We may support someone but we don't rob them of the ability to self-actualize by doing what they need to do for themselves. In my own experience, when I saw my friend or partner as having problems I thought I could fix for them, I didn't have to risk being as intimately known. In the role of caretaker, we can hide behind the guise of the fixer instead of being an authentic, whole person. It is a lot less vulnerable, but ultimately, it is a lot less rewarding, too, not only for you but for the other person, as well. Caretaking doesn't allow the other person the space to be who they truly are, because they see us as the problem solver and have no reason to take on the challenge of solving their own problems. Most importantly, when we assume this role, we are depriving ourselves of a sense of wholeness, too.

SARAH: *She takes a breath knowing it's totally okay that he doesn't fully understand her perspective right now.* Yes, exactly. Can we make time for each other again?

PATRICK: Sure, I did really enjoy those breaks. How about we meet for lunch on Thursday?

SARAH: Sounds great.

Notice Sarah's body language here in addition to her non-accusatory language. All of this helps Patrick relax and be more open to the conversation. We can't perfectly predict how the other person will respond in any conversation, but I encourage you to remember that this person is someone you are already in an established relationship with—or growing one with—so they almost certainly see you have value.

Learning to Let Go

In codependency, it may feel like healthy relationships are elusive, but to build intimacy first requires the inner commitment to emotional safety. While vulnerability is essential to intimate relationships, it is not appropriate to be vulnerable when we don't feel safe. When there is abuse, consistent disrespect of our needs or boundaries, lies, or other behaviors that lead to ongoing pain and anxiety in a relationship, the healthiest thing we can do is walk away rather than try to salvage the relationship. In our codependency, we may believe that we have invested so much time, energy, and care, so it's just a matter of time before this other person wakes up and sees our worth, but unfortunately, this is not always true. In our recovery toward becoming interdependent, we celebrate and honor that intimacy is fundamental to a joyful and meaningful life. However, we also honor

our authentic self and boundaries, and we cultivate relationships that are mutually healthy and intimate.

FOR YOUR MUTUAL BENEFIT

A healthy relationship benefits both parties. There is a balance
of giving and receiving. Of course, in a healthy relationship, we
don't keep score and things are not always perfectly equal. In
a healthy relationship, we give from a place of generosity and
unconditional love while trusting that because the other person
cares for us deeply, they will want to give back to us, as well.
At the same time, in a healthy relationship, we understand that
there is an ebb and flow to this relationship, where sometimes
we may be giving more or receiving more, depending on life
circumstances. If your spouse just lost their parent, there may
be a period of time when you are more of an emotional support
for them, and at other times, perhaps when you had an illness,
your spouse took more of the lead. We don't keep score, but
we know when a relationship is inherently imbalanced; we feel
exhausted, resentful, taken advantage of, or invisible. These
signs are important to identify and discuss. If the other person
continues to be unwilling to have a balanced relationship, this
is likely a relationship that doesn't serve your health.

DON'T FORCE IT

We often are told, especially when it comes to dating, that there
are tips and tricks to get others to commit. However, in truth,
there are just some people who have both the willingness and
the skills to have an intimate relationship, and there are some
people who don't. The latter group is not a reflection of your
worth. These individuals often have an avoidant attachment
style, which has been found to apply to about 25 percent of
the population. People with this avoidant style of attachment

perceive relationships as a nuisance and are resentful toward their partner. They can be difficult to get to know and very critical. Furthermore, they may repeat a cycle where they initially want an intimate relationship but then perceive the other person as burdensome, so they will end things or even "ghost" them. They may repeat this cycle with different people or the same person. Of course, a person with this avoidant attachment style can work toward secure attachment, but this is a process they must do for themselves, and because of the very nature of avoidant attachment, they are unlikely to be motivated to do this work for a long time. It is important to restate: There are people who have both the desire and the skills to maintain a healthy, committed, and intimate relationship, and there are those who don't. It is incredibly ineffective and painful to believe that you have the ability to heal the latter group. Your valuable time and energy is better spent investing in someone who also wants a relationship.

OWN YOUR POWER

It can be scary to walk away from an unhealthy relationship, but you have done so much to prove your strength in life. You are resilient. You have survived so much to get to this point and have started to recover—this is a celebration. One of the most painful but powerful skills is learning how to let go when necessary. Sometimes we must trust in ourselves to cope and learn to manage the healthy space in our life that is left when we end a relationship. Also, it is important to continue to cultivate other healthy relationships. A truth I have learned about pain is this: The pain of leaving a toxic relationship eventually subsides, whereas the pain of being in a toxic relationship continues for as long as we stay in that relationship.

EXERCISE: Appreciation and Gratitude

You may have discovered some relationships in your life are not sustainable, which can be a painful realization, but hopefully you are seeing some relationships have the potential to be intimate—or already are! For these existing relationships, a common barrier to deeper intimacy is resentment and holding a grudge. To begin to counteract the negative impact of resentment, it is important to tap into appreciation and gratitude for those healthy relationships in our lives.

For this exercise, think about all the people in your life with whom you have a meaningful relationship or there is potential for more intimacy. Contemplate and write down what you appreciate about them; identify at least three things. In Sarah's case, despite her desire for more intimacy, she appreciates that Patrick is a calm person, cares about providing for the family, and is intelligent.

When we focus on what we appreciate about someone, we may risk the vulnerability of telling them we appreciate them more. But it fundamentally changes the energy of the relationship. People can feel when they are appreciated or criticized, and it is human nature to shy away from the latter and embrace the former.

TAKE IT FURTHER

In this step, we discussed the value of intimacy and how it can lead to a satisfying and fun life in recovery. However, this process can trigger fears regarding abandonment or being smothered; it requires the commitment to lean into vulnerability while being authentic and maintaining healthy boundaries. It is in our intimate relationships that we can experience the greatest proof—and rewards—of codependency recovery. Learning how to be intimate is the final step of recovery, as it challenges us to be both self-protective and fully accepting of others.

As you move forward in cultivating healthier, intimate, and interdependent relationships in your life, please consider the following:

1. While often equated with romantic or sexual relationships, intimacy also includes closeness and friendship. These qualities can be cultivated in numerous relationships. At this time, continue to focus on the relationships you already have that bring joy to your life. Consider how you can interact more often with these people even in small ways. Also, think about how often you experience caring and healthy touch on any given day, and contemplate ways you may be able to give or receive more touch to help add joy and manage stress.

2. Healthy intimacy requires the commitment to choose authenticity and to lean into vulnerability. In codependency, we hide behind masks and walls, including walls of caretaking and walls of resentment. It will be frightening, at first, to say what you really think in an assertive manner and to be willing to not only share who you are but open your heart and mind to receiving the other person's thoughts and feelings. We can mindfully lean into vulnerability. We can learn to notice sensations, such as clenching our jaw or feeling tightness in our stomach, that show we are resisting vulnerability. Practice noticing these

sensations, and when you are with people you feel comfortable with, share your thoughts and feelings in that moment. With practice, leaning into vulnerability will become easier. Don't try to eliminate the fear of vulnerability—fear is a common and fundamental human emotion. Strive to learn how to better manage your fear, and don't let it sabotage your relationships.

3. You may have a nagging sense that one or more relationships in your life may be impossible to heal. After all, if the other person is not willing to respect your needs and boundaries, it's not possible to maintain a healthy, intimate relationship. Be gentle with this awareness. At this time, for any relationship you are contemplating ending, write an old-fashioned list of pros and cons. For example, what are the pros and cons of staying in the relationship and the pros and cons of leaving? Notice what this exercise reveals to you. As an aphorism credited to ancient philosopher Lao Tzu states, "New beginnings are often disguised as painful endings."

4. True intimacy requires us to be protected and honored in our authentic self, and it requires us to do the same for the other person. Part of your recovery involves learning how to be vulnerable and authentic while practicing detachment to fully accept the other. Consider this quote by theologian Thomas Monk: "The beginning of this love is the will to let those we love be perfectly themselves. . . . If in loving them we do not love what they are, but only their potential likeness to ourselves, then we do not love them: we only love the reflection of ourselves we find in them." Take some time to journal about your thoughts or feelings regarding this quote as well as your fears of what will happen if you accept your loved ones for who they are. Finally, journal about the potential benefits of making it a practice to choose to accept them.

Conclusion
Following the Path

Congratulations on working through this book! You have cou-
rageously started living an interdependent life. I hope you have
learned more about yourself and are discovering that you truly
do bring invaluable gifts to this world by being your authentic
and unique self. The world needs you in all your authentic glory.
Also, I imagine you are starting to notice some of the relief of
beginning to set boundaries and communicate assertively in
your life. Hopefully you are also feeling more connected to
yourself and to others.

The Steps: Important Takeaways

Recovery from codependency is completely possible with
consistent commitment to the steps of recovery. When practicing these steps, we notice we are no longer stuck. We are fully
awake and conscious in our lives, no longer waiting for external
approval or proof of our worth and our right to a satisfying and

connected life. It is important to note that no one step is more important than the others, as recovery relies on the practice of integrating all the steps so that these healthy activities and behaviors become natural in our daily lives. However, if you feel overwhelmed at times by the steps of recovery, I encourage you to maintain a daily focus on self-care first, as this practice allows us to maintain the strength to set boundaries, communicate assertively, and tolerate vulnerability.

STEP 1: GET IN TOUCH WITH YOUR "SELF"

In recovery, we want to learn how to be a tree that is firmly rooted so that we may stay grounded no matter what life throws our way. We stay grounded by being clear on who we are and what we value most in life. Therefore, when life becomes overwhelming, we will still be able to stand on our own two feet. We move toward this sense of being grounded as we reconnect and honor our authentic selves. The more we know who we authentically are, the more we know what we need from ourselves—self-care—and from others related to boundaries, communication, and intimacy.

At times, we may notice a sense of self-disconnection slipping back in, but this is not a moment of failure. Instead, this is invitation to practice mindfulness, the act of going within through deep breathing, yoga, meditation, or journaling. These quiet, contemplative acts allow us to hear our true self again.

Throughout our lives, self-discovery is an ongoing process. We are never done getting to know ourselves, just like we can never fully be done learning about someone else. You are dynamic and incredibly multifaceted. I believe that continuing the work to know ourselves is not only personally rewarding but also an incredible gift to the world. In our self-awareness we can live with integrity, and the true meaning of integrity is wholeness.

We can give of ourselves from a truly generous place when we feel whole. This sense of generosity has a healing effect on our families, friends, and communities.

Finally, self-awareness continues to deepen and transform our relationships as we continue to remind ourselves that the only person we can change is our own self. This willingness to change can powerfully shift unhealthy dynamics.

STEP 2: PRIORITIZE SELF-CARE

Daily attention to self-care is incredibly valuable in recovery, as this practice allows us to nurture and strengthen the roots of our metaphorical tree. Healthy self-care practices nourish us so that we can do the work necessary to live interdependently. Of course, there is no perfect way to care for ourselves, and it is very normal to return to unhealthy coping strategies, such as drinking or eating too much at times. This is not a failure but rather a reminder to notice where you may be neglecting yourself. Often, self-neglect is a result of deprioritizing the ways we care for our mental and physical health—the things that we enjoy and truly nourish us.

Noticing how we are nourishing—or neglecting—our physical and mental health and recommitting as needed to the activities that leave us feeling supported are an ongoing process. It is also important to remember that self-care is not a luxury; it is the natural order of life. Our bodies are designed to be active but also need rest, and our minds need time to problem solve but also to play and be creative.

STEP 3: BUILD BOUNDARIES

The cornerstone of codependency recovery is the commitment to setting boundaries. Without boundaries, we will continue to feel resentful and overwhelmed in life due to our own decision not to self-protect. This behavior sums up a lot of codependency; therefore, committing to advocating for yourself is fundamental to becoming interdependent. It is important to continue to stay mindful of what feels good for you in your life and relationships, and what leads you to feel taken advantage of or violated. The latter will clue you into boundaries you need to assert to self-protect.

Of course, even when aware, we are not always immediately ready to set a boundary. This is okay. It can take time to set boundaries, as this process can be frightening. Hopefully, over time, you have cultivated healthier relationships where setting boundaries is more natural, but it can take a while to get there. We cannot set boundaries perfectly, and healthy boundaries are inherently flexible, so they may authentically change over time or depending on the relationship. The important work when setting boundaries is to implement them when you are ready, and once you do, to establish consistent and clear consequences if others violate them.

It is important to remember that it is not selfish to set boundaries; rather, it is self-protective. Interdependency is about the balanced care of self and others, and without boundaries, we stay stuck in codependency. Setting boundaries is loving not only toward ourselves but to others as well, as it shows them how to have a healthy relationship with us free of bitterness and resentment. Finally, there may continue to be people you encounter who violate you after you set boundaries. This is not a personal failure or representative of your worth! Some people are just unable or unwilling to respect others, and this is information for you.

STEP 4: MAINTAIN OPEN COMMUNICATION

In codependency, it is very common to communicate indirectly or in controlling ways. We have a lot of practice in communicating ineffectively, and so learning how to practice communication skills requires patience and effort. We work on progress, not perfection, to create the sorts of interactions that are mutually supportive.

As we recover, we want to communicate assertively more often. When we communicate assertively, we say honestly and kindly what we think, feel, and need to share with others. At the same time, we balance this by recognizing every person we have an interaction with has the right to a very separate perspective; this is the basis of interdependency. We work on approaching our relationships from the perspective of being on a team together so that our interactions are focused on supporting one another rather than trying to "win." Negotiation is common in healthy interactions.

Effective communication is supported by self-awareness, self-care, and healthy boundaries so that we may know what we need, express this in a balanced way, and care for ourselves if disappointed rather than be critical or harsh. Therefore, to effectively communicate, we want to maintain our focus on the first three steps so that we can communicate assertively more often in the moment. Self-care and boundaries allow us to take breaks as needed, too, as it is important to remember that if we become too emotional (the sympathetic nervous system kicks in), we need time to collect ourselves (activate the parasympathetic nervous system) to communicate.

STEP 5: NURTURE INTIMACY

Human beings are designed to seek connection with others, as our survival has been dependent on it. A desire for intimate relationships is not codependent; rather, it is fundamental to a healthy and joyfully interdependent life. Furthermore, we now know one of the most important things we can do for our personal health is nurture our relationships. Research shows that social connection may be as important to our health as eating properly and exercising—if not more important!

As we recover, we remember that even while our culture may emphasize the importance of some relationships over others—such as the idea that a spouse is more important than a friend—this is not true from a physiological perspective. It has been found that people have great health risks even when married, if their marriages are disconnected. All types of relationships have the potential to be nurturing, and learning to focus on the totality of our relationships, including those with our family, friends, colleagues, and even people we interact with in our community—such as the barista at the Starbucks we visit—has benefits for our health. We are designed to need to feel like we belong to the community we interact with, and learning to turn toward others and be present and grateful in our interactions is transformative. Even a simple hello to a passing neighbor can shift our mood in a positive way.

Interdependency highlights that balance in our relationships is necessary. Balance involves give-and-take as well as mutual care for one another. When we have secure attachments, we are more confident in our lives. As you recover, though, it is important to remember that you cannot force health into every relationship you may encounter. Sometimes the most powerful gift we can give ourselves in creating healthier intimacy in our lives is learning to let go of unhealthy relationships. In order to better cope with these losses when they arise, it is important to continue to seek support from those who are present in your life. Moving from codependency to interdependency allows us to recognize that it is not selfish or burdensome to rely on others, and in fact, healthy people want to show up for us. Finally, learning to appreciate the ways we have support and healthy relationships is important. Noticing we have people in our lives to be grateful for can lead to feelings of vulnerability, but whenever we're faced with vulnerability, the healing path is to lean into it to enjoy what we have.

Manage Your Time

Recovery is not a final destination. It's an ongoing decision and commitment to the life we want to lead. We want to remember to schedule the little things that support us in our interdependency, such as a workout, a healthy meal, Skyping with relatives, and reading. In codependency, we often say no to ourselves by neglecting ourselves. We want to remember that saying yes to ourselves is not selfish but imperative for recovery. Recovery comes to us in every moment we show up for ourselves in a healthy and balanced way.

At this time, you may want to revisit your Self-Care Schedule (page 71) and update it, as you may be learning more about what actually works for you. You may want to remove something that you've discovered doesn't nourish you, and you may want to add new activities, too.

You're in Charge

Early in recovery, some people express the fear that they will regress to where they were when their codependency was at its worst. But that is not possible. Your recovery work has

Keep It Up

Change is a slow process. We cannot recover perfectly. Believing we have something to prove in that regard would mean we have more work to do on our negative belief systems. It is important to remember, too, that mistakes are part of change. This is how we learn and gain more information. Our missteps when we try to put our skills to use, such as when we communicate ineffectively, allow us to problem solve to continue to improve. Remember: progress, not perfection. Just by reading this book, you've started your change process. Furthermore, what I know to be true about change is that eventually this process builds momentum, and then, suddenly, it feels like everything is clicking into place in multiple areas of your life. The seeds you've planted, carefully tended, and been patient with suddenly sprout. That reward is worth the patience.

We must also remember to be patient with others, too. When we change, they experience change by proxy whether they wanted to or not. Our change means that they must learn new ways of interacting with us. Many people will be willing to do this work for the two of you to have a healthier relationship, but they may resist it at first or not have the skills. It is important to practice detachment. Even if the people in our lives change, too, they most likely will not follow the same exact process we did. That is okay; each person has the right to their own reality and to make their own mistakes.

inherently changed you. You can trust in your change. As the Greek philosopher Heraclitus is thought to have said, "No man can cross the same river twice, for it's not the same river and he's not the same man." Life will challenge you with situations that have the potential to harm, but as you recover, you interpret these new situations differently and respond with more skill. I encourage you to consider the changes you have already started making in your life that would have seemed impossible a year ago. You have already begun this challenging work.

We live in a world in which we are sometimes expected to stay quiet to keep others comfortable. This may happen on a small scale, such as with our families, or on a larger scale, when it comes to issues related to power and privilege, such as racism or sexism. We see this reality playing out when we see the truth tellers in our families or in our society being scapegoated and shamed.

As I recovered and tapped into my power, I often went back to this Madeleine Albright quote for support: "It took me quite a long time to develop a voice, and now that I have it, I am not going to be silent." It is revolutionary to claim our power in this world. The life you create is dependent on you. You're never stuck—maybe you need to reevaluate how you spend your time and what you are prioritizing, but you *always* have options.

I deeply believe in your power to recover, and I hope, more than anything, that you believe in yourself more deeply as you practice these steps. You got this!

Resources

The following books, websites, and support groups may be helpful resources in your recovery work.

Websites

My personal website, Dantia Wellness: www.dantiawellness.com. Articles on improving relationships, setting boundaries, and restoring a healthy sense of self, including positive body image.

Co-dependents Anonymous: http://coda.org. Information on the 12-step community for codependents, helps you find a meeting, and more.

Sex and Love Addicts Anonymous: https://slaafws.org. The 12-step community for "anyone who suffers from an addictive compulsion to engage in or avoid sex, love, or emotional attachment."

Mindful: www.mindful.org. Articles and podcasts on the benefits of mindfulness and meditation, as well as mindfulness exercises.

Tara Brach: www.tarabrach.com. Free meditations and workshops for more training.

Self-compassion.org. Test your level of current self-compassion, learn the benefits of self-compassion, and access exercises to increase your self-compassion.

Books

Facing Codependence: What It Is, Where It Comes From, How It Sabotages Our Lives, by Pia Mellody

The New Codependency: Help and Guidance for Today's Generation, by Melody Beattie

Codependent No More: How to Stop Controlling Others and Start Caring for Yourself, by Melody Beattie

Trauma and Recovery: The Aftermath of Violence—from Domestic Abuse to Political Terror, by Judith Herman

Waking the Tiger: Healing Trauma, by Peter A. Levine, with Ann Frederick

The Power of Now: A Guide to Spiritual Enlightenment, by Eckhart Tolle

The Gifts of Imperfection: Let Go of Who You Think You're Supposed to Be and Embrace Who You Are, by Brené Brown

Daring Greatly: How the Courage to Be Vulnerable Transforms the Way We Live, Love, Parent, and Lead, by Brené Brown

The Dialectical Behavior Therapy Skills Workbook: Practical DBT Exercises for Learning Mindfulness, Interpersonal Effectiveness, Emotion Regulation, and Distress Tolerance, by Matthew McKay, Jeffrey C. Wood, and Jeffrey Brantley

Attached: The New Science of Adult Attachment and How It Can Help You Find and Keep Love, by Amir Levine and Rachel S. F. Heller

Facing Love Addiction: Giving Yourself the Power to Change the Way You Love, by Pia Mellody, with Andrea Wells Miller and J. Keith Miller

Hotlines

National Suicide Prevention Lifeline: 1-800-273-8255 or TTY
1-800-799-4889. https://suicidepreventionlifeline.org

National Alliance on Mental Illness Helpline: 1-800-950-6264.
www.nami.org

National Domestic Violence Hotline: 1-800-799-7233 or TTY
1-800-787-3224. www.thehotline.org

Rape, Abuse, and Incest National Network Hotline: 1-800-656-4673.
www.rainn.org

References

American Psychological Association. "Social Isolation, Loneliness Could Be Greater Threat to Public Health Than Obesity." *ScienceDaily.* August 5, 2017. http://www.sciencedaily.com /releases/2017/08/170805165319.htm.

Beattie, Melody. *Codependent No More: How to Stop Controlling Others and Start Caring for Yourself.* Center City, MN: Hazelden, [1986] 1992.

Beattie, Melody. *The New Codependency: Help and Guidance for Today's Generation.* New York: Simon & Schuster, 2009.

Berman, Robby. "Your Brain Interprets Prolonged Loneliness as Physical Pain—Why?" Big Think. January 6, 2017. https://bigthink .com/robby-berman/the-powerful-medical-impact-of-loneliness.

Brown, Brené. *Daring Greatly: How the Courage to Be Vulnerable Transforms the Way We Live, Love, Parent, and Lead.* New York: Avery, 2012.

Coelho, Paulo. *The Alchemist.* New York: HarperOne, 1993.

Chopra, Deepak. *The Path to Love: Spiritual Strategies for Healing.* New York: Three Rivers Press, 1997.

Davis, Daphne M., and Jeffrey A. Hayes. "What Are the Benefits of Mindfulness? A Practice Review of Psychotherapy-Related Research." *Psychotherapy* 48, no. 2 (June 2011): 198–208. https://www.ncbi.nlm .nih.gov/pubmed/21639664.

Elsevier. "Loving Touch Critical for Premature Infants."
ScienceDaily. January 6, 2014. http://www.sciencedaily.com
/releases/2014/01/140106094437.htm.

Freedman, Jill, and Gene Combs. *Narrative Therapy: The Social
Construction of Preferred Realities.* New York: Norton, 1996.

Fuller, Julie A., and Rebecca Warner. "Family Stressors as Predictors
of Codependency." *Genetic, Social, and General Psychology Monographs*
126, no. 1 (February 2000): 5–22.

Godman, Heidi. "Regular Exercise Changes the Brain to Improve
Memory, Thinking Skills." Harvard Health Blog. Last modified
April 5, 2018. https://www.health.harvard.edu/blog/regular-exercise
-changes-brain-improve-memory-thinking-skills-201404097110.

Gottman, John M. *The Marriage Clinic: A Scientifically Based Marital
Therapy.* New York: Norton, 1999.

Hadhazy, Adam. "Think Twice: How the Gut's 'Second Brain'
Influences Mood and Well-Being. The Emerging and Surprising View
of How the Enteric Nervous System in Our Bellies Goes Far Beyond
Just Processing the Food We Eat." *Scientific American.* February 12,
2010. https://www.scientificamerican.com/article/gut-second-brain.

Holt-Lunstad, Julianne, Timothy B. Smith, Mark Baker, Tyler
Harris, and David Stephenson. "Loneliness and Social Isolation as
Risk Factors for Mortality: A Meta-analytic Review." *Perspectives
on Psychological Science* 10, no. 2 (March 2015): 227–37.
doi:10.1177/1745691614568352.

Johnson, Susan M. *The Practice of Emotionally Focused Couple Therapy*,
2nd ed. New York: Brunner-Routledge, 2004.

Komagata, Nobo. "Attachment and Non-attachment: Attachment
Theory and Buddhism." Last modified November 30, 2010. http://
komagata.net/nobo/pub/Komagata09-Xtachment.pdf.

Krossa, Ethan, Marc G. Bermana, Walter Mischelb, Edward E. Smith, and Tor D. Wagerd. "Social Rejection Shares Somatosensory Representations with Physical Pain." *PNAS* 108, no. 15 (March 28, 2011): 6270–75. doi:10.1073/pnas.1102693108.

Lapakko, D. "Communication Is 93% Nonverbal: An Urban Legend Proliferates." *Communication and Theater Association of Minnesota Journal* 34, no. 34 (Summer 2007): 7–19. https://cornerstone.lib.mnsu.edu/cgi/viewcontent.cgi?article=1000&context=ctamj.

Levine, Amir, and Rachel S. F. Heller. *Attached: The New Science of Adult Attachment and How It Can You Help You Find and Keep Love.* New York: Penguin, 2010.

Levine, Peter A., with Ann Frederick. *Waking the Tiger: Healing Trauma.* Berkeley, CA: North Atlantic Books, 1997.

McAfee, Tierney. "Nancy Reagan's Romance with Ronald 'Was Probably More Important Than Their Love for Their Children,' Says Friend Larry King." *People* Magazine. March 9, 2016. https://people.com/celebrity/inside-nancy-and-ronald-reagans-romance-and-its-impact-on-their-children.

McIntosh, James. "What Is Serotonin and What Does It Do?" *Medical News Today.* Last modified February 2, 2018. https://www.medicalnewstoday.com/kc/serotonin-facts-232248.

Mellody, Pia, with Andrea Wells Miller and J. Keith Miller. *Facing Codependence: What It Is, Where It Comes From, How It Sabotages Our Lives.* New York: HarperCollins, [1989] 2003.

Mellody, Pia, with Andrea Wells Miller and J. Keith Miller. *Facing Love Addiction: Giving Yourself the Power to Change the Way You Love.* New York: HarperCollins, [1992] 2003.

Merton, Thomas. *No Man Is an Island.* London: Hollis & Carter, 1955.

Moyer, Christopher A., James Rounds, and James W. Hannum. "A Meta-analysis of Massage Therapy Research." *Psychological Bulletin* 130, no. 1 (January 2004): 3–18. doi:10.1037/0033-2909.130.1.3.

Murray, Michael T. "You've Heard Gratitude Is Good for You. Here's What Science Says." Mind Body Green. Accessed September 28, 2018. https://www.mindbodygreen.com/0-18054/youve-heard -gratitude-is-good-for-you-heres-what-science-says.html.

Rollins, Nancy, Joseph P. Lord, Ethel Walsh, and Geraldine R. Weil. "Some Roles Children Play in Their Families: Scapegoat, Baby, Pet, and Peacemaker." *Journal of the Academy of Child and Adolescent Psychiatry* 12, no. 3 (July 1973): 511–30. doi:10.1016/S0002-7138(09)61261-9.

Ryan, Kelly. "Five Ways Junk Food Changes Your Brain." RMIT University. September 19, 2016. https://www.rmit.edu.au/news /all-news/2016/sep/five-ways-junk-food-changes-your-brain.

Satir, Virginia. *The New Peoplemaking*. Mountain View, CA: Science and Behavior Books, 1988.

Schnall, Marianne. "Madeline Albright: An Exclusive Interview." *Huffington Post*. June 15, 2010. https://www.huffpost.com/entry /madeleine-albright-an-exc_b_604418.

Siegel, Daniel J., and Tina Payne Bryson. *The Whole-Brain Child: 12 Revolutionary Strategies to Nurture Your Child's Developing Mind*. New York: Bantam Books, 2011.

Simone, Nina. "You've Got to Learn." *I Put a Spell on You*. Audio recording. Philips, 1965.

"Timeline Stories." Al-Anon.org. Accessed August 30, 2018. https:// al-anon.org/blog/timeline/aa-wives-meet-together.

"Timeline Stories." Al-Anon.org. Accessed August 30, 2018. https:// al-anon.org/blog/timeline/letters-sent-87-groups.

Von Teese, Dita. "You can be a delicious, ripe peach . . ." Twitter post. September 6, 2010. https://twitter.com/ditavonteese/status/23210190813.

Watzlawick, Paul, Janet Beavin Bavelas, and Don D. Johnson. *Pragmatics of Human Communication: A Study of Interactional Patterns, Pathologies and Paradoxes.* New York: Norton, 1967.

Williamson, Marianne. *A Return to Love.* New York: HarperCollins, 1992.

Winfrey, Oprah. "The Powerful Lesson Maya Angelou Taught Oprah." Oprah.com. October 19, 2011. http://www.oprah.com/oprahs-lifeclass /the-powerful-lesson-maya-angelou-taught-oprah-video.

Zantamata, Doe. *Quotes about Living.* Iko Productions, 2014.

Index

Acknowledgments

Learning to recover—to become interdependent—requires the support of other people, and I am deeply grateful for those who have taught me that interdependency truly is attainable.

To Amy Haller, I must start by thanking you because every healthy relationship I have ever experienced started with you. Prior to meeting you at age 11, I did not know that any two people could have a truly loving, supportive, and unconditional relationship. Relationships, at best, were temporary safe havens but quickly became tumultuous. However, you understood me and even when, in my codependency, I acted in strange ways, you stood by me. More than any other human being, you know the depths of despair and self-sabotage my codependency drove me to, but you never stopped believing in me and reminding me of my worth. There are no words for how grateful I am to you for teaching me that unconditional love and support are possible. The relief you feel that I recovered is humbling and reinforces just how you love me no matter what.

To Alexandra House, you entered my life in adulthood when I still deeply believed that the possibilities in life were finite. I did not know that I could develop a deep best friendship in my adulthood, and becoming so close to you has expanded my sense of what's possible in this world in incredible ways. After all, our friendship is what has allowed me to create one of the greatest dreams of my life: having our own private practice! The deep intimacy we share has taught me that family can be expansive, too. All the things we share—including a home—made me realize family is truly not just about bloodlines. You are my sister. Thank you so much for all your support and feedback that helps me become a better person. I am so grateful for all the countless times that you have provided a shoulder to cry on in the face of loss and someone to dance with to celebrate the successes and joys of life.

To my Nana, while our relationship did not survive, I am forever grateful for the encouragement I received from you growing up. You deeply nurtured my love of learning and my passion for writing. You had been deprived of many opportunities, but you greatly celebrated mine; you took me to countless lectures, book signings, and writing workshops to support my dreams. You always emphasized the importance of an education and self-reliance. I deeply believe that although you didn't know how to break the deep generational patterns in our family, you saw my potential. Thank you for helping me understand that I truly am capable of standing on my own two feet.

To my editor, Nana K. Twumasi, thank you so much for choosing to embark on this journey with me. Your guidance has immensely clarified my perspective, and this partnership with you is allowing me to accomplish the very first dream of my life: to write a book. Thank you so much for your guidance, clear vision, and understanding. I became a therapist to help others heal, and it is awe-inspiring to recognize this project of ours can help so many! Thank you.

To my Princess Kitty, you were my furry best friend and loyal companion for 13 years. Caring for you faithfully and seeing myself through your eyes allowed me to begin to finally see my lovability and worth. You were incredibly special—and particular!—and if you loved me, there must be something worthwhile inside of me. Your passing during the writing of this book was deeply painful, but I realized that through our incredible bond, you helped me break through the final questions about my worth and strength. Loving you made me strong and losing you made me realize it. I love you so much, little girl. Thank you.

Last but certainly not least, I must thank my mother, Catherine. We have truly experienced both codependency and recovery together. There are no words for the depth of loss in our family we experienced together when we decided to finally stand up for what we believed to be right. The courage you showed in learning how to be healthier to be the matriarch of our family is incredible. Your commitment to healing allowed you to finally become present and start to understand me. This has been an incredible gift and allowed me to appreciate you and understand you more fully. Having a healthy and connected relationship with you was a dream of mine but one that didn't seem possible for many years. Thank you so much for your own healing and the way you fiercely love me. You showed me that with love, commitment, and acceptance, relationships can be fundamentally transformed into something better than one could ever imagine. I dedicate this book to you, as our relationship proves recovery is possible!

About the Author

Krystal Mazzola is a licensed marriage and family therapist who has been fascinated by relationships and the potential for positive change since she was a child. While attending graduate school, Krystal learned about The Meadows, a world-renowned treatment center, and set a goal to work there eventually. A few years later, Krystal met this goal and fully discovered her passion for helping individuals recover from codependency. Krystal was also able to fully enter and maintain her own personal recovery from codependency with the support of others. From this place of deeply knowing recovery is possible, Krystal now provides individual and couples therapy at the private practice she co-founded, Dantia Wellness. Krystal lives in Phoenix, Arizona.